HEAVEN SCENT

Celebrating The History of the Welsh Songstress

Cheryl Beer

Published by Parlor Press

Firt Impression 2005
ISBN

© Parlor Press

For Lilian Conner, My Guardian Angel

Dedicated to the late Siwsann George
& all women, past and present,
who have enriched our culture

Bridgend Print Cente

PREFACE

Written by Moira Andrew

You'd think it would be a simple combination – Wales and song – that they'd go together like leeks and laverbread. Well it's no problem if you're born a man, an enormous hurdle if you happen to be a woman.

It is this common experience that Cheryl Beer explores in these pages, *Heaven Scent: The Welsh Songstress.* The girls can climb the first rungs of the ladder with ease, especially when they are young and fresh-faced, slim and pretty. Sure, when they are no threat, the boys are delighted to see them fronting their bands, bringing that touch of glamour to their gigs.

It is as the girls become women, especially if they are serious singers in their own right, that the difficulties mount. As Heather Jones says, 'For me, being a woman, I think it's been a barrier.' The men always want to be not only top of the bill, but 'top dog' in every way, even in their personal lives. Boyfriends object to their women being in the public eye, 'I wouldn't want any wife of mine to be in the Radio Times.'

And when they are married and pregnancies come along, the women are forced first to leave the stage, then to start from the bottom again once the children have grown up. By this time, of course, the women are no longer young and this too, brings its problems. They say, 'It's the young ones, still in their twenties, they want.'

Cheryl, herself a talented singer/songwriter, brings many of these frustrated Welsh songstresses to life and in this book she allows them to tell their stories in their own individual voices. There are tales of struggle, of lost confidence, of final success against the odds.

There is a great deal of fun in the anecdotes too – tales of childhood in wartime, of the closeness of Welsh village life. As Beattie says, 'In and out of each other's houses, the door always open and we'd all help each other out.' Cheryl and her eloquent contributors dust out the shadowy corners of a forgotten way of life in the Valleys.

'Oh God, it was a hard life. A terrible hard life. It was hard times when you didn't know where the next meal was coming from.' But with the help of their music and their singing, the women win through. Not always to international, or even national success, but sometimes simply to working through the Arts Council or taking part in singalong sessions in hospitals and old people's homes where they are thoroughly appreciated – if seldom making big money.

What shines through each of the stories that Cheryl Beer has brought to us, is the tenacity and dedication of these women, their joy in relationships, in life itself and, of course, in their singing. Despite all their difficulties, they don't – and won't ever - give up, certainly not while Wales echoes to their voices.

MARIA JANE WILLIAMS

By kind permission of The Williams Family

CONTENTS

Heaven Scent: Celebrating The History of The Welsh Songstress

HEAVEN SCENT

Lyrics & Music by Cheryl Beer
In celebration of the contribution made to song by Heather Jones

I sat next to an angel, we were one
I listened, she sung
Eyes closed, souls rising
I held onto her wings
As we flew
And just so I knew
That this was no dream
I wondered down stream
To fields laced with Heather

And the song of an angel is Heaven Scent
The voice of an angel is Heaven Scent
Lullaby of an angel

Lips coloured with lyric
Her cheeks blushed with the rush
Of heart beats beating
No rest until
The perfume of her voice
Had f a d e d

And the song of an angel is Heaven Scent
The voice of an angel is Heaven Scent
Lullaby of an angel

She opened her angel eyes
And I could see
She did not know the journey
Nor where she had taken me
But I knew it to be true
For in my heart grew
Fields laced with Heather

And the song of an angel is Heaven Scent
The voice of an angel is Heaven Scent
Sweet Lullaby of an angel

CHERYL BEER

WHO IS CHERYL BEER?

I wonder that myself sometimes! After living in the Glamorgan area for 21 years and longing to move to the countryside, I have finally been drawn to the beauty of West Wales. Now, rather than waking up to a bustling high street, I am tucked away in an old stone cottage, listening to blue tits singing in my garden.

Music is my life. It always has been. My Mum says that I could sing before I could talk and dance before I could walk.

I'm not going to delve too deep into my life because this book is not about me. I just want to give you some insight into why I would become interested in preserving the history of women and their contribution to song in Wales.

For almost all my life, I have written and performed songs, either in bands or touring a One Woman Show. The media has, over the years, focussed on my womanhood and how *unique* I am, touring solo with my own songs, describing me as *one of a kind*. When I read about other women singer/songwriters, the same line is taken in their editorial. Surely we can't all be the first! When I began searching for my history, I found the library to be full of books about men's contribution to the world of song, hardly ever a mention of women and certainly not *welsh* women. I think the final straw was when Pat Smith showed me a book on Celtic women musicians, which had been published recently, and we couldn't find even one Welsh woman listed. I was astounded. 'So,' I thought, ' is it true? Do we have no history? Or is it that our history is strangely silent and just needs a platform from which to be heard?'

Having a first degree in Behavioural Sciences and a Masters in Women's Studies, my experience as well as my instinct, told me that something was afoot. I started to ask around. Most of the older musicians that I knew were men. A friend of mine, Jeff Rees, who worked with me at the Ogmore Centre Trust, on a creative writing course for children, gave me a list of contacts that he felt would be able to help me. One of the contacts was a 70 year old Jazz musician, who has sadly passed away during this research. He told me straight that *women in the old days weren't as they are now. They didn't want careers and it was enough for them to have their husbands and their homes.* Mmmm!

I started to toy with the idea of carrying out wider research, which would enable me to find women who were singer/songwriters in the *old days* and record oral histories with them. From their oral histories, I could unearth the truth about women's contribution to song in Wales. It then dawned on me that I could write songs about these women and put together a new One Woman Show, where audiences would be informed about women's lives and their contributions celebrated.

How exciting! Just a few problems; how would I find the women and how on earth would I afford to spend all that time working on it? It would take me years and I needed to meet these women now, while they could still tell me their story. I wrote a proposal and discussed my ideas with the Arts Council for Wales, who advised me to put a bid together. I sent off for the forms and got cracking! Don't get me wrong, applying for funding is a time consuming process, but it really makes you think things through and is an excellent way of getting completely focussed. I was successful and got a small grant. I couldn't believe it. It gave me the freedom to put aside half my working week for the research and to write the show. The rest of the week I carried on performing, facilitating song workshops, and presenting for radio and/or festivals: anything to make up my wage.

At first, it was very slow. I couldn't find any women to interview and I started to lose hope. I put adverts in local magazines, doctor's surgeries and old people's homes, but to no avail. Down spirited, I thought I would re-visit the library and search for other women who had been on similar quests, to see if I could pick up any tips. While there, I happened upon 2 lines in a book about a woman from Neath Valley, who, in the 1840's, had interviewed women over 70 years of age from the valleys, collecting welsh folk song history. I was so inspired by this woman *Maria Jane Williams*. I could not believe that I had found a woman from Wales, who had successfully carried out her work over 150 years before me. Her goals were so similar to mine. If she could do it, against all the barriers and stereotypes she must have faced, then surely I could find women too.

The librarian was fantastic. We searched the database only to find that in the archives she had a copy of a book that had been written in memory of Maria Jane, a re-issue of her work. I was so excited. It was better than waiting for Santa on Christmas Eve. The librarian called me up just a few days later. I must have run to the library. As I opened the book, there on the front page, was a full-scale picture of Maria standing with her harp. I could not believe the realization that came to me as the tiny print at the bottom of the page became clear.

When I originally sketched the idea for this work, I was renting a flat at Llanharran House. It is the most beautiful manor house set back from the road and butting onto the forestry commission .The servant's quarters and barns have been converted into flats. My flat overlooked the untouched cobbled courtyard from one end, and a field of pot belly pigs from the other. The Williams family were most kind. Yes, the *Williams* family!

The print jumped out at me, a portrait of Maria Jane Williams, hanging at the family residence: *Llanharran House*. My skin bristled with goose bumps. From that point, I have felt that I was almost meant to do this work, that I am continuing a tradition, a women's tradition of song in Wales. Perhaps the very reason that the whole idea came to me, was precisely because I was staying in the home of the Williams' Family, playing my guitar and writing songs where the portrait of Maria hangs. Maybe she had been waiting for me. I found myself getting quite carried away with the idea!

Fully charged up and motivated, I decided I needed to think laterally. If I could not find women of 70 years plus, perhaps I might find women in their 50's or 60's who would know of, or remember women that I could contact.

Some years ago, I was performing at Cyfartha Castle in Merthyr and on the same line up was *Calennig*, a folk band from Llantrisant. There had been a woman in the band called Pat Smith. She and Mick Themes had been running the folk club in Llantrisant for years and I thought she might be a good person to get me started. I telephoned Pat and she couldn't have been more helpful. She and Mick gave me a long list of names that might be able to give me advice. When I got home, I realised that Pat's life in itself was an amazing story. It was meeting her that motivated me to change my brief. I was funded to find 5 women of 70 plus, but I decided that any women I met on the journey would be included in my work, as their lives give valuable insights too.

I carried out oral histories with 20 women, although I talked to and met many more than this. The only reason they are not all included is because we either could not match up diaries, or they made a decision that they did not want to take part. I have made no value judgements as to whether or not someone's life should be celebrated. I contacted every name I was given and if they agreed to be included, then that was enough for me. They are all very different types of women with different backgrounds. Some were born in Wales; others have lived here for some time. Some are welsh speakers; some are not. They live in very different parts of Wales and are from different genres of music. Having said that, they also have a lot of similarities and I will say more about that later.

Thanks to the grant from the Arts Council of Wales, I was able to write the show. Now I had to think about putting it together as a tour. Alongside the performance, I set about writing workshops and seminars to accompany the show, so as to take *The Songstress* to the heart of the community. I submitted a second bid and had another small grant to help me produce, market, rehearse, promote.... I wanted to promote the tour in a way that gave back to womanhood, so I came up with the idea of releasing a fundraising single *Heaven Scent*. All the monies from the single are donated to breast cancer research, Velindre Appeal.

My oldest friend, Caroline Spencer, died of cancer last year and she was treated at Velindre, the only specialist cancer research hospital in Wales. To my mind, there was no more fitting charity to support.

Saving Women's Lives as well as Preserving Women's History.

Joining me on the single are Heather Jones, Ruth Exell-Stevenson, Kate Strudwick, Linda Simmonds and Sian James, all of whom kindly contributed their time and their wonderful music, with Jeff Beer and Gwyn James giving their engineering skills. As for folding 1000 CD covers and putting them in the plastic wallets, that was down to a team effort between myself, Jeff, my Mum and my sister Gemma. Bridgend Print came up trumps, donating the design and printing costs.

It dawned on me halfway through my research that the oral histories would make the most amazing book. A show is a fantastic celebration, but a book is forever. A book is a reference point for other women who, like me, want to know about their history. The photographs and the oral histories would give another platform for women's voices to be heard.

Sounds easy, doesn't it? All I had to do was transcribe the interviews and stick them with the photographs and I'd have a book. WRONG! I have lived, breathed, slept, and dreamt *The Welsh Songstress*. Edits and re-edits and more re-edits. Then there's the sticky topic of who is going to pay for it all! After talking to different publishers, despite their support and interest, I decided that if I wanted this to be done, then there was only one person that I could rely on to do it my way! ME!

So, I have set up my own publishing company **Parlor Press**, and self-funded this publication. I have done this because I believe it is of paramount importance to save our history and to save it in a way that celebrates these women. It has become my quest! And what is money after all? However, I'm sure this is a question that my bank manager wishes I had a much more straightforward answer to!

All that said, I have trawled the library for other people's oral history books; I have surfed the Internet for more hours than I've spent sleeping, to find a formula that I feel best celebrates women's contribution to song. I'm not saying that it's necessarily the best formula, but it's the one I feel most ethically comfortable with.

It seemed to me that other presentations of oral history predominantly tended to break up the text and use it to emphasize themes and concepts. This is an excellent technique for presenting the common themes in people's lives and giving an overview of the social context. I have broken up text like this myself for my theses and dissertations in the past. However, for *The Songstress*, I felt strongly that breaking up the women's stories to emphasize themes and concepts, would result in losing the sense of the *whole* person. When you read this book, I don't just want you to get an insight into women's history of song in Wales. I want you to *meet* these amazing women in their homes, the same way that I did. I don't want them to be *lost* in the text, but *found* in it. I want you to get a real insight into the person, so that you get an overall sense of their personality, how they have lived their lives and experienced their individual pasts. By doing this, I hope that you gain a sense of how the personal can be political, in the way life experiences are shared in different contexts.

There are very obvious themes that link these personal histories: like how motherhood has affected the women's careers; their relationships with their husbands and partners; career breaks; stereotypes they have had to overcome; pleasures that they find in music; reasons why they feel being welsh has influenced them; how their lives may have been different if they were men. I feel that had I broken their text to emphasize these concepts and themes, you may have lost the sense of them as whole women. I hope that by reading about their life as one whole piece, you will get a sense of something greater than the parts of their lives.

You may, as I have, identify with these women's experiences. As the author, I have not overtly analysed nor debated the political position of women within the social context of song. The fact that the history of *The Welsh Songstress* has remained strangely silent in itself speaks volumes. The reader can make up their own mind by listening to what these women tell us about the past.

Every effort has been made to ensure that the women who have taken part in *Heaven Scent: Celebrating The History of the Welsh Songstress*, have had the opportunity to view, comment upon, discuss and amend their oral histories and the songs written about them. This has presented some interesting difficulties for me in terms of methodology. Oral history is a snapshot of a person at a certain time in their life. For example, one songstress felt that she had been *a bit down* at the time of the interview and that she wanted to change her script to represent her new found happiness. Another did not quite understand the concept of oral history and felt that I had left my essay about her unfinished, nor could she quite take on board the fact that the text was comprised of the words that she had said and not the words that I had written about her. I have tried to accommodate these requests, and others made by some of the other women, without compromising the nature of oral history for the reader. After all, the idea of *The Welsh Songstress* came from a place inside me where I was tired of being erroneously written about.

As the author, I do not necessarily share all of the views, opinions and comments expressed by the women. Neither can I guarantee that the content of what they have said is 100% accurate. There are few 100% guarantees when relying on the human memory. What can be said to be true for certain, is that this book has given *The Welsh Songstress* the opportunity to speak about and record her life experience, as well as her contribution to song, in her own words.

I just want to add that I am in my back bedroom now, typing this book and it is in this back bedroom, that I have recorded the songs for the fundraising single, edited the transcripts, written the show, applied for funding … It's just me… Little old me.. And it could just as well be you too! If you have something that you really want to do, but you think you're too old, or too weak, or just *too*, then I hope my work inspires you to believe that ordinary women can do extraordinary things with their lives, and that sometimes what we believe is ordinary is actually wonderful.

The Welsh Songstress has taken over my life and there have been times when I have wondered, 'Why am I doing this?' But then I remember Maria Jane and I think of all the amazing things that women have achieved and are achieving in their lives. I smile to myself knowing that I have to carry on.

I was truly inspired by the women I met whilst writing this book and I thank each and every one of them, not just for taking part, but also for making a pathway for other women… for women like you and me. When I started this research, I expected to find quiet, elderly ladies in nursing homes that *used to* sing. That's why I couldn't find any! They are *still* singing, performing, organising, and living their lives through song. Thank you for teaching me that it isn't all over at 40 and that, all things being equal, I have a lifetime of song ahead of me.

A Gift for You ...

... I have included a gift for you. It is a CD at the back of the book, which I have edited from the oral histories and recordings of the women singing. I am hoping that by hearing their voices it will help you to connect with them even more.

Peace, Harmony and Good Health!

Photograph donated by Miss Betts to W.I.T. By kind permission of Jen Wilson, Director of Women in Jazz, Swansea. Showing the mother of Miss Betts in an all-woman travelling guitar troop, circa early 1900's.

Please Note: Photographs are donated from personal collections. Therefore reproduction quality may be effected.

Footnotes:
Cambrian Minstrelsie (Avalon Gwalia) Vol.1 Parry.J & Rowlands.D, T.C & E.C Jack Edinburgh 1893
Ancient National Airs of Gwent and Morgannwg Maria Jane Williams. Introduction by Daniel Huws. Welsh Folk Song Society 1988

HEATHER JONES

HEATHER JONES

Introduction

Heather must be one of Wales' longest, continually touring Welsh women singer/songwriters. Song has been her life and her true love throughout good times and bad. Heaven Scent is the title track from my One Woman Show and it is the song that I have written to celebrate the work of Heather Jones. Whilst sitting next to her at her dining room table, she took me on a journey, singing with a voice that I can only describe as the perfume of angels. As a mark of respect, the respect she feels she does not ordinarily receive, her life history is presented first.

I always had a mother in the kitchen singing the alto parts to everything imaginable. From The Messiah to Ivor Novello songs. So there was always music around. She's always singing, even now, and she's eighty-five.

There was a talent competition in Cathays High School where I went, and nobody was going in for the singing. Now, I didn't know that I could sing. I didn't think I could sing. I wanted to be a pianist you see – a concert pianist – so I was going in for the piano. And one of the teachers said to me, 'Now, your mother sings in a choir. Get her to teach you a song. Somebody has to sing on this stage.'

And I said, 'I can't sing.'

'Now, you do as you're told and tell your mother to teach you a song.'

So my mother taught me this lovely song, called *Sing Joyous Bird*. My piano teacher came along to the talent competition and I froze in the middle of my piano performance. I looked at the audience and I ran off crying. I was only eleven and I was very small for my age, so I looked about seven.

Anyway, after that it was, 'Oh well, you know, I've lost that. I haven't won the competition.' So I went on singing and I brought the house down because they couldn't believe that a little girl had such a big voice.

After that, that's when I had lots of attention, which I hadn't had before because I'd been so small and ill. I had terrible asthma and I was never picked to be a milk monitor and all that. This gush of attention I thought, 'Wow! This is great!'

The Welsh teacher got me involved in the Eisteddfod and that was when I was eleven. I was in all the Eisteddfods. I did a duet with a girl, but I couldn't stop giggling. So I wasn't really taking it seriously. But in

1964, I went to a lovely Welsh place up in North Wales, to the Urdd Camp, all the youngsters go. Everybody had a guitar and I wanted a guitar. So I think for my fourteenth birthday I had a guitar and it turned out that I wasn't bad at playing. I then started to accompany myself instead of getting the pianist to play for me. And of course then I just fell in love with the folk song thing that was happening, like Bob Dylan and Joan Baez. I was in a group with a couple of girls. We were called the *Eirlysau*. One of the girls was called Eirlysau and she was going out with my brother.

We had another group before that and we all played guitar. That one went on television. I went on television; first I had to go for an audition. We did a concert in the *Reardon Smith* with a group called *The Beti Wyn Choir* and she used to have various people doing little bits and because I could play the guitar she thought, 'We'll have something different here.'

The man from the BBC, Doctor Meredith Evans, was in the audience and he asked me to go for an audition. I was only fifteen. I was a bit nervous, but I went. And then the next thing I knew, I was on was my first television programme. I was sixteen by then, and it just sort of went on from there really. There was always something happening. I had ten guineas for that television programme and I went straight out and bought a dress. And I'm still doing that now. I'm a shopaholic.

I was sixteen and I had my picture in the Radio Times. I was going out with this boy from Ely. He saw the picture and said, 'I wouldn't want any wife of mine to be in the Radio Times.' And I realised then that it was going to be a struggle to be a singer and have a private life. He wanted to be top dog I suppose, isn't it? You know a lot of men are like that, aren't they? He wanted to be top dog and he didn't like it that I was. He said, 'I don't want other men looking at my woman.'

'Oh, I'm going to have a lot of trouble with this one,' I thought.

Anyway, in the meantime I'd been liasing with a guy called Geraint Jarman, who was a poet and he was keen on me really. He kept calling at the house. In the end, I finished with this guy from Ely and started going out with Geraint. We formed a partnership of writing songs together. He would write the words and I would write the tunes. We'd go to folk clubs and there was a poetry club in Cardiff called *No Walls*. I'd go there and play the guitar for him to read his poetry to other people. It was a really exciting sort of era. He was Welsh- speaking so he got me really into the Welsh scene and away from the English scene. My parents didn't speak Welsh, so I was going down the English track until I started going out with him.

Then I went to college to be a teacher, but after a year I left because there were so many engagements all over Wales. My father could see that I was earning money and he knew I hated college, so he allowed me to leave. I met a guy called Meic Stevens, Mad Meic. We formed a group, me, Geraint and Meic. We were going all around Wales doing concerts and television and records. We had a ball touring around for a year.

In 1970, I had my first child, which was not planned, obviously. I mean, Geraint and I had to get married rather quickly and that sort of held me back a bit really. But Meic came round the house one day and he could see how miserable I was, because I didn't really want to be a housewife and a mother, just stuck at home in a house that I didn't like down in Roath. We had mice and we had snails coming through, oh it was horrible.

Anyway, he went back to the BBC to the club where he used to drink quite a bit. Got thrown out of there quite a few times – Meic that is, not me. And somebody rang me up and said, 'We'd like to offer you a programme.' So I had a series with a singer called Bryn Williams and I was his guest every week and did a song with him. About, a year and a half after that, I actually had my own series, which was quite big for a girl of twenty-two, who'd learnt to speak Welsh. It was a lovely experience and I had all these lovely clothes that I could wear. That was quite prestigious for me to do that. It was the first time a rock/pop group had been on Welsh television. I'd got *James Hogg* from Bridgend.

I'd never had a manager. I'd turned my back on all those sorts of people because I suppose I was a bit hot headed. I didn't think that anybody could manage me. I suppose I was doing so well it didn't matter really. And then they sent some of my tapes from the BBC to BBC Pebble Mill in Birmingham. They asked me to go up there for an audition for Pebble Mill. They actually used my audition piece for the very first Pebble Mill at One. I was watching it and thought, 'Blimey, that's me! If I'd have known, I'd have worn something a bit better.' I had just an ordinary jacket on. I was quite shocked they hadn't asked me back to do it properly. I got three months of that. I can't believe I did it live. I would die now. I had to do all sorts of things, walking through the grounds and sitting on a swing and having to sing as well. No miming or anything. I thought that might spring board, I might be spotted and something nice might happen to me. But it was a new thing, dinnertime television and most people didn't watch it. The only people who ever said they saw me, were retired people or women who were at home with their kids. It came to an end and that was that. I came back to Wales and went to join *The Caricature Theatre* in Cardiff, singing again.

One of the girls lived in London and she was part of a group called *Redbrass*. She said that there was an opening for a girl singer and did I want to audition. I went up and I got in and ended up touring with them for about three years. Unfortunately, we didn't earn much money. I remember we used to get thirteen quid per gig, which in '77 wasn't very much. You had to pay for food out of that, and your drinks and everything, so we didn't have much left. But it was an experience and I got to meet Annie Lennox. She came to the group. She's younger than me obviously, and I had to be on the auditioning panel for her.

They liked her and I liked her as well and we got quite close actually. She was a lovely girl, she is a truly lovely person. And she used to work on Camden Market. She had a stall there of clothes and she used to bring me all the tiny clothes because I was minute then. I was about six stone, something like that. And she used to bring me all the little size 8 clothes and say, 'Oh you can have this, because I can't sell it. Nobody's that small.'

I've still got those upstairs, some of those things. I don't contact her any more because she's big and famous.

Then I had a little bit of a dip in my life, because my father died and that really hit me for six. Then my marriage broke up to Geraint as well, so it was a bit of a low time. By now Geraint had started to play with my rock band and he'd become very, very popular and famous. It's like as if we overtook each other. One minute I was at the top, having my own series and he was just a jobbing actor, who couldn't get any work, and then suddenly we went like that … and everybody wanted him and he didn't want me anymore.

I found that quite hard to take, really. I'd lost my confidence. My father dying shot me to pieces and I had a bit of a nervous breakdown, nervous depression. I decided to get out of the Welsh scene and auditioned for a cabaret band called *Wine and Roses*. I passed the audition and that's where I met my second husband, Dave. He was the drummer. I had to pick him up every day and take his drums and him up to the gigs. We just got closer and closer. I was with them only for a year, but I'm still friendly with them.

I think I realised that my true love was the Welsh folk singing. I tried to make it back into the Welsh scene. It was like I had to start from the bottom again and work up. The first programme I had in '82, I was a backing vocalist for some guys that had never heard of me. It's like they'd forgotten me.

There were all these new youngsters. Caryl Parry Jones was in and everybody loved her. She was the newest thing, an excellent singer and musician and actress and poet and everything. She just had that bit extra that we didn't have really. So then it was just back to doing my usual dinners and concerts.

Of course I had Sam, my son, and that sort of took it out of me a bit, because my daughter was pregnant as well, so we had two babies... five months apart. I looked after the both of them for a while, until it became a bit too much. And then I had Megan, my eleven year old as well. I was in my forties with these two little babies.

I couldn't really take it seriously because I had these two children and the granddaughter as well. Then, in '97, I was offered again my own series, which was brill.

I'd had to build up this career again and I mean, there weren't many girl singers my age doing it really. They'd all given up. The only other one who'd really made it was Iris Williams and she'd gone. So, anyway, I did the series. It wasn't terribly well received. A lot of things went wrong. It was all a rushed job, unfortunately, but still, you know, I still had a lot of television work after that. It brought me a good whack of money and put me back on the scene again really.

I started singing with my daughter and a friend of mine called *Sioned Nair*. She's about forty-five and Lisa, my daughter, is thirty-three. They were backing me on songs and I thought, 'Gosh, these three voices sound good together.' So we've formed a group out of that and we still do work. Not an awful lot.

I've also forgotten to mention that in 1982 I started with a traditional Welsh band and we went to America in '92, when I was pregnant with Megan. Getting the plane, I had to run through the airport with this great big bulge. They actually pulled me out in Philadelphia, because I was pregnant and carrying a guitar. I was the only one from the plane that was searched. Of course, they didn't find anything.

I was asked two years ago, by Robin Huw-Bowen, if I would like to join with Eiry Palfrey and form a little group to go to America. So we went to America last year and did a tour of loads of different places.

I've done a lot really. I must write it all down one day. I went to Canada in '96 as well, on my own, and that was lovely. I didn't have a fee but it was a lovely experience to go there and meet everybody and see the countryside.

My husband doesn't seem to mind – well he does really. When I came back from America last year he didn't speak to me for a couple of weeks. You know he wasn't happy about it, but I think he's realised that I want to do what I want to do, and I'm going to do it. You can't turn down invitations to do things that are going to colour your life, so I do them.

For me, being a woman, I think it's been a barrier. I think it's because I'm not a particularly strong woman. I'm better now than I was, but when I was in my twenties and thirties, I wouldn't say boo to a goose.

I do some concerts and there's a guy on the bill who's not as well known as me, but I am still under him. I'd still find that now. And it really bugs me. I think, 'Well, hang on, I've been in the business now all these years, surely I could have a little bit of ...' but no. I don't know whether it's because I'm a Welsh learner, or what it is, but I don't feel as if I get the respect that a person of my age and experience should ... I should have something a bit better. I'm not a go-getter. But you can't change a personality. You know, I can't grab things. I'm not like that. I'm a bit of a pushover. You know, a bit soft.

I've managed okay, but that's only because I've lived with two different men who've been able to help me buy the house and all that. You can't really make a good living out of singing in Welsh. You've got to have something else to do. I mean, it's like Meic Stephens is so popular, everybody loves him and his work is always on the radio, but he lives in a council house in the dockland area. He just can't afford a house because we just don't get the big money.

I also sing in hospitals and old people's homes and that's really, really hard work, because you sing for an hour and talk all the time, going round with your guitar and singing and talking. It's exhausting and I don't get paid an awful lot for that. But, on a bad month, eight of those are better than nothing. I'm not getting the exciting work that I used to have. And I miss it really.

People say that I am singing just as well now as before, so therefore I feel it must be because of my age. Record companies seem to focus their energy on young girls in their twenties. I really feel as if I've been kicked in the stomach.

I don't have any future plans, really. I always just sit around and see what happens. I suppose if the day comes when there's nobody ringing, I probably would make an effort to go out there and find work. I don't think I'll ever give up unless I felt my voice wasn't good enough. There always seems to be something in the distant future.

It's lovely being with other people and working towards something. A theatre show ... I'd like to do more of that I think, but I would never go for an audition. I never go and put myself up for anything. I've also been doing a schools' project, going into schools and teaching Welsh traditional songs. That sort of sparked off other things. I'm going into MIND, we're having singalong sessions as well, so maybe it will be more like helping the community. I think that's my future. I still do the gigs on my own, if somebody wants me to do a gig. I do some work with Frank Hennessy now and again. Just appear on his shows. I enjoy that.

I would have liked to have worked with the bigger names, Joan Baez, Neil Young, and all those. I would like to have done backing vocals on their records. I mean, I may not have been good enough for that really.

I was friends with Iris Williams. I went with her on her very first journey when she passed her driving test. It was absolutely horrendous because she had a Morris Minor and it was before the A470, so we were going to Aberdare through Pontypridd. We were stuck at some lights and she couldn't get the car going again. We had to get blokes behind to push us, so that we could get the car going. I'll never forget that, it was funny. We used to travel together. We did duets and everything.

We got friendly through the Welsh scene I suppose, and we started going to a spiritualist church together. We went to this spiritualist church one day, on a Sunday, and there were only about ten people there. We were the only two youngsters. They were all in their fifties, sixties, probably. And there were five of them on the stage and they were giving messages to people. And they said,

'We have a message for the two young girls at the back.'

Then she said, 'One of you will become a very famous singing star.'

I thought it was me. And Iris, she thought it was her. And of course it was her!

Heather Jones

HAWYS GLYN JAMES

HAWYS GLYN JAMES

Introduction

Before his retirement, Roy Sear worked for many years at the museum of Welsh Life St.Fagans. I visited the museum to listen to recordings of songs stored in archives, recorded by Roy, with women from the valleys, to preserve welsh folk songs. I telephoned Roy to talk with him about my work and he kindly helped me by sending a long list of women whom he thought I could contact. Two of those women agreed to be interviewed. The first was Hawys Glyn James from the Rhondda.

Hawys has a very special aura. She has a gentle, kind face and a voice that sings, even when she is talking. Hawys and Glyn, her husband of 50 years, welcomed me into their home like old friends.

My mother was quite a pleasant singer. She used to sing folksongs and hymns, always when she was working. My father, who was a coal miner wasn't a singer, but all his family were very musical. My grandfather could play the organ and other instruments, so I've always been steeped in music. I can remember, thinking back to my junior school days, it was full of music, we were always singing. We'd spend the whole afternoon singing, and I loved it. So I've always been very, very fond of music. It's been a major part of my life really.

In those days, there was some idea that to get on in the world, you had to speak English. People thought that Welsh was useless to you. Although my parents spoke Welsh as a first language to one another, they didn't speak it to us. We're four in the family and only I speak Welsh. I was very fortunate in having two teachers who really inspired me. There was one who was a wonderful pianist and folk singer. My mother bought me the guitar that I used all through the years. She paid quite a lot for it. It was she who paid for the guitar for me and it's still in very good condition. My mother's great wish always was that I should make a record. 'You must make a record, you must. Oh! Please, make a record,' and I used to say, 'Yes Mam, next year now, when I'm less busy,' but I never got round to it.

I met my husband, Glyn, when I was competing in the Urdd Eisteddfod. He heard me singing and then he pursued me. There was a by-election over in Aberdare. Gwynfor Evans, the President of Plaid Cymru, was fighting a by-election, so Glyn found out by some means, where I lived. He knocked at the door and asked if I would come and sing. First of all I sang at the inaugural meeting for Gwynfor Evans. Then Glyn had the idea for me to sing on the loudspeaker. So we used to go round the streets. I made up songs about the election. Well, we'd stop the car in the evening, above Aberdare Mountain, and I'd sing. So the voice was going all over the valley. Afterwards, we were married within about 4 months. I think we were married through singing. My son, Telor, sings and plays the guitar and my daughter, Delyth, is musical.

I didn't know of any women, at that time, playing the guitar, but I went for lessons. Of course, I was teaching in the school opposite our house. It was a secondary modern school and I was teaching Welsh as a 2nd language, Drama and English. There was very, very little material at that time. So, I started writing songs for young people, isn't it? Simple Welsh songs to start with, and then I wrote more bilingual ones, giving a background to the children of their heritage, local stories and so on. I think I must have taught hundreds of children to play the guitar. For two or three years I had classes of teachers in the Teachers' Centre, and I taught teachers to play the guitar. Naturally, I used my own bilingual songs. You can imagine, the students thought I was really trendy. There was me playing the guitar, and going around performing. When I think of it now, there weren't women then performing with a guitar. Mind, I can remember in the chapel, at first, some of the members were not at all happy about it, but our own Minister was all right. I used to take groups of girls from the school and we'd do a whole service on a Sunday with the guitars. Lots of the girls got married in that chapel and they had no real connection with the chapel, except through me taking them there.

My mother lived in the next street and my sister-in-law and sister lived nearby with their children. My sister's a lot older than myself, so her children had grown up more or less. I was very lucky that they used to come here, and baby-sit. I had a free hand. My husband and I have been to Brittany with the Celtic Congress, and to Ireland and to Cork, where I sang with Sian James accompanying me on harp. We were in Patagonia, Argentina, about two years ago. I did some singing there. Not long after, on one of the digital T.V programmes in the evening, a girl from Patagonia was singing one of my songs. I've had letters from Australia, Ontario, all over, informing me that my songs have been sung.

As I say, I write ballads, hymns, all sorts of songs, patriotic songs, everything you can think of. Even as a child I had the ability. I've always been able to write poetry. They were very simple poems when I was young, and then I set them to music myself. I've always been able to do that. Sometimes, I hear a tune in my head when I'm in bed. I've always kept a little tape recorder near the bed. If I think of a song in the middle of the night and I can't go back to sleep because I can't get it out of my mind. I just sing that little tune into the tape recorder, because I will have forgotten it by the morning. Lucky that Glyn's a heavy sleeper. He doesn't take any notice of me at all.

I always wanted to publish, and fair play, my husband has always been like the wind beneath my wings. He always said, 'Oh! Yes, we must publish.' To date, I have 5 bilingual songbooks. I enjoyed being an artist going about, but my main purpose was for children and young people and grown ups to have an interest in their own country of Wales, to know their heritage, because I think that it's very important. I've written a Heritage book but we've sold out of them. So we're currently going to do a reprint. I've written so many more poems and lyrics that I can include in the re-print of the book. One of the poems is about the Rhondda. A young man, who was disabled through an accident in the pit, has written a book and he asked would I write *The Ballad of Trehafod* so that he could include it in his publication. I wrote the poem, including images from the early days, when the squirrels used to go from tree to tree, right up to the present time. When it was the Golden Jubilee, the Queen came to the Heritage Park. A copy of the young man's book was given to her. She came to speak to my husband and myself and asked why we were there? I said, 'Because my husband was the Mayor of the Rhondda and also, in the book that you have been given, I've written the song at the beginning.'

The Queen said, 'Oh! Very good. I shall read it with great interest.'

I said to Glyn, that night she might have been singing my *Ballad of Trehafod*. Well, you don't know, do you?

Glyn was councillor for 32 years, Borough and County. When he was Mayor of the Rhondda, we used to entertain in the Mayor's Parlour. I used to get some of the girls I'd taught in the past to come over and entertain with me for the whole night. It was like a cabaret, everybody wanted an invitation. I enjoyed it very much. Our adopted charity was Llwynypia Hospital. To raise money for eye treatment, we collected £28,000. I did a lot of singing for that! I did a sponsored sing here in the house and anyone could come in all day. I sang 100 of my own compositions, and we collected £28,000 to buy that eye laser.

Glyn, has been more than supportive. You'll be surprised when I tell you this. In one of my books, the publisher couldn't print music, so my husband did all the music by hand. Can you believe it? It's perfect almost. It had an award, at that time, with the Arts Council. Glyn's greatest sorrow in life is that he can't sing at all. Most people can keep a tune. Well, he can't. He can't even sing *Hen Wlad Fy Nhadau*. He says he can't sing because he never heard singing at home. Although he can't sing himself, if I were going to a concert, I'd say, 'Oh, I'm not sure what to sing tonight,' and he'd say, 'Let's think now, go over the songs… That's the one for tonight.'

And do you know, he was right every time.

I considered it the biggest honour in my life when I went into the white robes in the National Eisteddfod because that's the highest order .You can only get there by invitation You can't try any examination. So, my husband and I are in the white robes.

Is there anything else that I would have liked to have done? I've got tapes, but I've never had anything official. I always said I wanted to get round to it, but I never did. I don't know why. I always thought 'I'll do it next year,' but it never came, did it? And at this age now, I don't think I will make that record. I had to retire from school because I had nodules on the vocal chords. The specialist said, 'No, you'll never sing again' but the speech therapist said, 'Yes, you'll sing again' and my voice came back as clear as it always was. I think probably, at that time, I would have made tapes, but this all happened and I think it put me back a bit.

I've taught people who are in their 60's now, because when I first started teaching I wasn't much older than them, I was only 22. They come to me and say, 'You inspired us to send our children and our grandchildren to Welsh schools. We liked Welsh so much with you because you presented it in such an interesting way, that we wanted our children to have the opportunity to learn our language.'

It's amazing what you can do, isn't it? Like a pebble, the influence spreads, and then it gets wider, you don't know where it's going to end do you?

Songstress Update

Hawys and Glyn celebrated their 50th wedding anniversary this year. After meeting them and listening to Hawys's life history, I agreed with her Mother that she should have *done a record!* I thought it would be a real surprise to collect some of her recordings from cassettes that she had and with the wonders of modern technology put them through my studio at home to make a CD/ album for them.

Autumn Song: A Collection by Hawys Glyn James contains her own compositions and a traditional folk song. I burnt 50 copies, boxed them up for her and took them up the Valley. They were so pleased that they even mentioned the CD as part of an interview with the Rhondda Leader.

With a little bit of extra effort, we can make each other's dreams come true.

ANITA WHITEHOUSE

ANITA WHITEHOUSE

Introduction

Anita and I talked at length by telephone initially. She was an absolute hoot and the pair of us couldn't stop laughing. When she came home to Wales, visiting family and friends, we met up. I don't know why, perhaps because she had such a contagious laugh and strong voice on the telephone, but I had conjured up this image of her in my head as quite a big person. So when a tiny, white- haired woman opened the door, I wasn't sure if I'd got the right house! As soon as she smiled, I knew I had.

Oh my God, I couldn't contemplate a life without song. Music, love it, love it. I'm eternally grateful that my mother put me to the piano when I was little, because that's very helpful for a singer. You haven't just got to learn it by heart; you can read it.

I grew up in the Rhondda Valley, a place called Trealaw. I went to grammar school in Porth, which is a mile or so down the Valley. In my Infants school and Junior, I was taught in English. There was no Welsh in the Rhondda Valleys when I was little. Interestingly enough, my father spoke Welsh and my father's sister and brother. My mother, on the other hand, from a bit higher up in the Valley, spoke only English. A fortune-teller once told my mother, out of the blue, 'Put your daughter to music.' I'm not a believer in that sort of thing at all, but being as I was musical, and not too daft, she got this piano.

I always feel my father had some Italian blood in him because he had the most fantastic voice, and his sister could sing and his brother. I remember my daughter made a tape for my mother of all the great tenors for her to play. She was living in sheltered accommodation then, and a couple of weeks later I went down to see her. When I got down there a fortnight later she said, ' Oh, put that tape on Neet.'

'Yes alright Mam.' I remember my mother said, 'Oh! don't he sound like our daddy?' I thought, 'Yes Mum.' There was something, it wasn't as big a voice as Pavarotti's, but that ring, that Italianate ring.

Interestingly enough my son Paul has got a really good singing voice. In one of his shows he sang as a cockney. There was Harry Enfield in the sketch, telling him to do this, that and the other, trying to teach him a pop song. Paul couldn't get it and then all of a sudden he said,

' Yeah, but it's not proper singing mate' and suddenly whoosh!

He was singing this Italian aria. It was actually him! He could have been a singer I'm sure, but he was too interested in the fun of life. He's got a natural voice. I think in a funny way you're partly blessed with it and then you're lucky if you get good advice and good knowledge because voices can be damaged.

Although I could sing as a youngster, when I was 14 I had my appendix out and when I came out of hospital, I couldn't sing.

After that I didn't bother. Then I got married and we were getting our home together. One day I was in the bathroom singing and Harry, my husband, who was a very devoted music lover with a marvellous ear for singers and music, he said to me, 'Gosh Neet, that's good, go on.' I was listening to Kathleen Ferrier singing and I was singing with her. When it got to the top note I stopped you see. Harry said, 'Oh! Come on Neet, you can do that.' The next time it came round I sung it and he came into the bathroom and said, 'My God, that's fantastic, you must come to my singing teacher for lessons.' So I did. I went to his singing teacher down in Cardiff and had lessons. He actually trained me as a mezzo-soprano and I was in the finals of the Golden Voice of Wales. In fact, I was then accepted in the chorus at Covent Garden as a mezzo-soprano but I was potentially a soprano.

I was very lucky. I was doing a concert in Wales just before we went to London and this wonderful woman was in the audience. Her name was Julia Helger. She had sung at Covent Garden. She was Hungarian and at the end of the concert she came up to me and she said, 'Darling, you must not sing in the chorus at Covent Garden. You are not a mezzo you are a soprano. You vill come to me tomorrow and ve vill vork.' You can see how it's imprinted on my memory 50 years later.

She was an amazing teacher. She taught a method called *Gesprachgesungen*. The aim is to sing without unnecessary effort and I'm sure that's why I've kept my voice. I went to what they called *The Opera School*, which was connected to Covent Garden, where they trained young singers. I was lucky and met a wonderful man called Norman who was at Covent Garden. Bless his cotton socks, he was a big fan of mine, and he used to take me to his own home to coach me. I began to sing soprano and from then on, I sang most of the great roles as it were. You never know, do you, what's going to happen in life.

I was about 24 years old, but then I had my two children and I stood back from it for a little bit. I sang with the Welsh National and I feel I was just lucky considering my first priority was my children. They came first. In the end I gave up singing because I was travelling too much. I didn't want to be doing that and leaving the kids. I'd been told if I wanted to do the big roles, which I loved doing, I'd have to go abroad and sing them first to be invited back to Covent Garden. By this time I'd decided I was going to give it up because I wanted to be more with the children. I'd been invited to Germany to sing a leading role but I'd have to have gone over there for three months rehearsing, so that's really how I gave it up in the end. For me, my children were a greater priority. All that travelling didn't seem right. It began to wear me down a bit.

I was 35, that sort of age, you know. I can remember singing with Tom Allan, Sir Thomas Allan now, and we did the requiem together. I was Rosetta and he was the baritone. I often think, 'WOW! He went on and did all those roles at Covent Garden.' I could have sung Michaela, but by this time I had already planned to go into teaching, and because I'd been a professional, I only had to do a year's study. I went into primary school to teach and I loved that. I loved it, so I feel I've had a bit of the best of both worlds in a funny way.

I was very lucky because I taught in a school very near me. I taught there for 20 years, same school. You can see how adventurous I am! I taught Special Needs in the end, and I loved that, helping kids to read. I've had a number of wonderful pieces of feedback from that.

One day two boys knocked on my door, 'Oh!' I said ' Oh! Adam, John.' I hadn't seen them for ages. They were little kids when I'd taught them and here they were big boys. John had told me he was going to go into the army. I said, ' Oh! lovely, you look after yourself, love', and they started nudging each other. 'Go on, you say.' 'No, you say.' Anyway in the end, Adam said, 'We've come, Mrs.Whitehouse, because we wanted to tell you, if it weren't for you we wouldn't be able to read.' A friend of mine was in the kitchen making a cup of tea and she said, 'Good God, that's better than a standing ovation at Covent Garden!'

I had a nice little choir in the school. We did music and movement but in general I actually taught in class. Later on, I took on Special Needs because I just worked out a way of helping them to spell. English is so difficult for some children. They can be very bright but if you haven't got a good visual memory, spelling English is very difficult. I know so many languages and there's not one language as difficult as English for a child to spell. It used to hurt me a bit to see quite clever kids battling with spelling. I realised that you could save kids a lot of worry and angst. In fact my daughter had a bit more of a difficulty with reading than my son, and yet she's got a degree now.

I was walking down the road near where I live, a couple of months ago now, and this woman was going, 'Mrs Whitehouse, Mrs

Whitehouse.'

'Oh,' I said, 'Mrs Bergam.' She used to help me with Special Needs when I was teaching.

'I've just had a phone call from Michael.'

Michael Bergam was her son and I'd taught him. He'd had some difficulties with reading and spelling and he'd just rung her saying, 'Please go and tell Mrs Whitehouse, I've got my doctorate with honours, and if it wasn't for her I wouldn't have had it.' Isn't that touching? I mean, he might have made it eventually, but I helped him to make it without feeling it was too difficult.

Now I teach singing up in England a bit. I don't do much teaching. I'm very tired now for goodness sake. I get people who come recommended. I don't charge. I just do it for the love of it. I love passing on knowledge. The reason I feel I can still sing is because I discovered a very lovely, easy technique. Now, I teach my pupils just four exercises and once they've practiced those and perfected them, then you've got your voice for life. How did I stumble on it? Well, it started with Julia Helger. She would just make me sit down, and if I were to move a bit she would go, 'Oh no darling, keep the voice in the bed.'

The Germans call it *spoken singing* and that really helped tremendously. But of course, it was very difficult to go and have singing lessons. I had my own two children, I had my adopted son, and I had an aunt living with me, and the cleaning and cooking and everything. I mean, they were helpful but I was in charge of it, as it were. Then one day we happened to be in *Foyles* and I was looking in the music section. I saw this book about the very same method of voice production. I was reading it. Harry came over. ' Oh what's that? Gosh,' he said.

I said, 'Oh! It's fantastic.'

He said, 'Love, you could buy it if you want to. You haven't got to digest it all now.' We laughed and obviously I bought it. It somehow made a lot of sense to me, but I do know an awful lot of people who've read it and misunderstood it, then overdone it. I've managed to simplify it.

I began to realise that English speaking people, English speakers up in England, have difficulty singing the *ah* vowel because it goes onto their throat. Now the reason the Italians and the Welsh sing so well is because they are actually resonating the voice in a different area, in the cheekbones, you see. I keep saying, 'I must publish it, I must get it down,' and one of these days I probably will. Perhaps my son will because he's used to filming and things. We did a quick run through but it needs to be rehearsed.

I'll tell you, it's ever so funny actually, when we were rehearsing what I'd do for the film, I wanted to show how relaxed you can be singing, because literally, I can sing lying down. So, I sort of went back and when we looked at it, I looked a real slob laying back in the chair. We said, 'We can't have that on there mate.' It's been a bit of fun. I must get it done, I must. They really are wonderfully simple exercises and they keep the voice healthy for life. All this business of open your mouth wide, it's bad you see. Sorry they got it wrong! Watch Pavarotti, he doesn't move when he sings. He hasn't got his mouth wide open singing, 'Aaaaaahhhh.' Now this is why the Welsh are so lucky, like, *'cause they talk like that see,* which is very helpful for singing. If it becomes Anglicised it's no good. As I say, I probably will get a video out. Somebody recently did a singing exercise video with her husband: *You too can sing* Carrie Grant, I met her not so long ago. She was introduced to me actually, because we were at a show that her children were in. I knew the conductor. I don't advertise to teach singing at all, but if I go to a concert and hear somebody messing up their voice, and it's a good voice, I've got to go and say, ' Come to me for 6 months and ve vill put it right,' like I had done to me.

My lad, who's a bit of lad and a bit of a comic, shall we say, we were discussing it and he said, ' I know how to put your voice forward, mother,' and he sort of lunged forward and he said, 'You go like that, don't you?' I thought, 'Yeah, that's right, love'.

But what does it mean? How can you push without damaging?

You can keep relaxed. It's about doing it with a deep sense of relaxation.

Being Welsh, it's a very necessary underpinning. Every singer should be Welsh or Italian .Oh gosh, I still feel Welsh. Well, look how many years I've been up there and you can still hear my accent. Oh yes, it's something you never loose. I love coming back. Recently I was with *my little lad* as I call him, Keri. We were in Neath. I was so touched. We went and had lunch and met the friendliness of people. It's so obvious that everybody is really friendly, smiling to that one and this one. It was quite touching really. There was a man on the corner of one of the streets playing a trombone and I think everyone stopped. He was fantastic; he was begging really, but he was absolutely fantastic. Just about everybody stopped and gave him something *en passant,* and I've seen that in London with beggars. They sit and nobody gives them a penny. I know it's a different thing, millions of people in London and lots of beggars, but it was very different I felt. The atmosphere in Neath, I thought, 'Oh gosh, yes, sometimes I miss this, 'but I'm lucky where I live, I live in a very friendly little cul-de-sac.

After a cuppa Anita and I move to the piano for a song …..

There were one or two pianos in the street that I lived in, not every child by any means. I used to go to somebody for lessons, not very far away, just down the road and round the corner. I went to her and enjoyed it really. It's been such a support.

I can play for you now. The only thing is this piano is very out of tune. It's a wonderful piano. It's a good, good piano, but it's terribly out of tune. What do you want? *I could have danced all night,* or a couple of Welsh songs? Don't listen to my playing whatever you do! Ah, Sweet Mystery. Look, *I Could Have Danced All Night. Wedi Teithio'r Mynyddoedd:* a bit of Welsh. This is a lovely little song: I haven't sang it for years. The piano is so out of tune, I won't sing out of tune, I promise…..

Anita sings so beautifully that I can feel tears in my eyes.
This tiny, delicate songbird sitting next to me on the piano stool, sings with the whole of her body and mine. When she has finished she turns to me….

Not bad for an old bag! I always say that. We always say that about my singing! I didn't record 'till I was 60 years old. I was too busy working and teaching I think. I was 60 when I made this CD. It was ever so funny. I sang 7 arias, and after the 6th or 7th the producer said, 'Anita do you want to come and hear these?'

The pianist and me were used to doing a recital. As we walked in he said, 'How do you do it?' I didn't know what he meant. I said, 'Pardon?'

He explained that recently he'd done a recording for a very famous pop singer. She took twenty-two takes for one item and she's very famous. I won't tell you who, I wouldn't want to.

I said, 'Well, you could think she was a perfectionist and I don't care a damn, if you like.' He said, 'Oh no fear, there's nothing to correct on them. I just thought you wanted a rest and to hear what you've done.'

My second CD is called *Still Singing at 70.* Do you know, I just feel very privileged in the life I've had, really.

women's jazz archive

JEN WILSON

JEN WILSON

Introduction

Whilst I was in Africa, the Director of Chard Women in Music, Angela Willes, gave me Jen Wilson's name as someone that she thought I should contact regarding my research. Angela and I were part of a group of British women attending the launch of Zimbabwe Academy of Music and Dance, of which we are both patrons. When I returned from my work in Zimbabwe, I tried to contact Jen but had no luck. Some months later, by chance, the operator gave me the telephone number of the wrong organisation and it happened to be Women in Jazz, where Jen is the Director. I couldn't believe my luck.

There was always music on in the house all the time and when I was growing up the radio was always on. Growing up in late 40's and through the 50's, every music programme seemed to have a little sort of jazz interlude. Like *The Goon Show* for example, always had a jazz section in the middle of it. My parents always had the radio on. They used to dance *The Charleston* to the records on the scullery floor because their feet used to make a noise. My brother, who's 6 years older than me, he was a drummer. He started building up a drum kit on tin boxes and cans. Anything to make a noise really.

It was automatic that I went on the piano because in those days, you always had a piano in your front parlour. And so it was, you gravitated towards it and bashed it and made a noise. I would play boogie for my brother. I managed to learn that. I taught myself by ear. My parents sent me to proper music lessons from the age of 6 and I quit when I was 12 because it was the sort of thing where you were encouraged to take the piano grades and piano exams. I used go to my piano teacher and say, 'There's this jazz record we're playing at home.' You just didn't do things like that in the 50's, it wasn't done to do things like that.

I found myself playing in the jazz club at the age of 14, in Swansea, and I should never have been there because it was a licensed premises. My parents, God rest their souls, didn't know what was going on half the time. If they'd realised that their little girl was sneaking off there, in amongst all these blokes! I remember having my first gig at 14 and it wasn't a gig really, it was more, 'We'll put Jenny on at half time.' I did my showing off boogie pieces. Then my brother, realising that I was beginning to sound not bad, he'd come down and fix his drums up and say, 'Play this faster, you're not playing this fast enough.' That's how I learnt how to play fast. It was improvisation I was interested in. As soon as you've got the basic idea of what the piece of music was doing, I'd bang my way through the chords. Once I'd got the chords right then I was away. I didn't need to look at it anymore.

There weren't any other young women like me. There were one or two singers who were then in their 20's, but I never, ever saw any instrumentalists coming through the jazz club. The only one I ever saw was Kathy Stobbart, who came with Humphrey Littleton to Swansea and did a big concert. I thought, 'Wow! this is a woman player.' Years later I ended up interviewing her.

It was all so patronising when I look back. You learn your feminism through being patronised. My God, putting up with all that. I used to play in the jazz club where they would say things like, 'You shouldn't be playing things like that, you should be playing things like pretty ballads.' Or, 'Why don't you play this pretty song instead of hammering the keyboards like grim death?!' But I always wanted to play like I wanted to play.

I was about 16 and we ended up having various bands depending on which day of the week it was. So if it was Wednesday, it was *Jenny and the Giants* and if it was Friday, it was *The Tony something or another quartet* or whatever. There were quite a few name changes of the band depending on what we were doing. Then I was asked to join a more mainstream band who were well known, *The Tempos*. We had no equipment. There were no PA systems to cart round, because there weren't any. It was only big popstars that had amps and things. The rest of us managed without. It was different in those days. All venues had a piano. They could be a bit, sort of, crap. Sometimes they were grand pianos if you were lucky with your venue, not like today. The boys in the band went off to University. One *had* to get married I think and there were a few scooped up by women. I did a lot of solo piano, which was very good for learning how to play and how to put a bass line on when you were by yourself. Then I got married and went to live in London in a flat, which obviously didn't have a piano in it. I looked up a lot of jazz in the clubs and bought loads of records and all the rest of it.

There was an interlude then of kids and all that stuff you've got to cope with.

I started playing again in the mid 70's. I didn't stop playing, obviously, but it was difficult with bands. I used to keep my hand in with local jazz clubs and the odd gig that came along, but I didn't form a band. It was always problematic really. My husband was a social worker and sometimes he was out all night. I think from the mid 70's to the 80's I started getting back in with various bands and things like that and I've ended up making a CD when everybody else is retiring. Making a CD at this late stage in life!

I got a job as an administrative secretary at Swansea University, Adult Education Department, and they had a music tutor there who was coming up to retirement. It was a job that grabbed my attention and I thought, 'Here we are as a secretary and one doesn't go applying for tutorships.' There's what we refer to now as the glass ceiling, which was very definitely just above my head. I was still a musician in the night and I started putting on things like guitar workshops. I started running a part time class in the evenings. Whilst I was still a secretary, I did a course in the evenings running 20 weeks: *Blues Women*. It was looking at the lives of women and playing their records. I did quite a lot of research for that. I asked the Prof. in the department if we could run it as a course. He said we could if we had enough people.25 turned up in a pub room. I did a few of those courses and because that was successful I organised a guitar day school. I did the first guitar day school on a Saturday and 55 guitar players turned up. It was a bit of a shock.

I thought, 'Well, shall I apply for the tutorship?' I didn't tell a soul. I didn't tell the Prof. I didn't tell my typing colleagues. I told nobody. They were looking for somebody who could work in the community on the music side, but also they opened the job up into a performing arts tutor. I thought I'd have a bash, and put the application in. I went back to work on the Monday as a secretary typing away. So, time went by, another two weeks, three weeks and then I had a letter to say I was short-listed. Get real! I thought it was obvious I'm not going to go any further. This is fantastic, I've got this far. I thought, ' I'm not going to get the job because you're going to get professional musicians coming in.' I was chuffed. I was thrilled, without any help from anybody. I went to the interview totally and utterly at ease. I didn't have any collywobbles. I wasn't nervous at all because I knew I wasn't going to get the job, but I was going to do a bloody good show for all the other secretaries who've never had the opportunity to get this far. The other applicants were all soaking with sweat, waiting their turn to go in. I would assume the guy from the Welsh National Opera was going to get the job, but I got it. It was great. I started the job and it was absolutely brilliant. I was lecturer in performing arts, which was music, dance, drama and video.

At home we couldn't move for the jazz archive I was building up and I thought the department could house it. Prof. said, 'Oh, well if you get funding, I'll house it.' And of course he thought I'd never get funding in a million years. I turned up one day with 2 cheques totalling £17,000 from Arts Foundations. They gave me a big room in one of the big houses that they own, just outside the main campus building. I moved in and ran my operations from there. For those 2 years and half of the next year, it was absolutely brilliant. Then universities became cost centres. The last year in the university was an absolute nightmare. There was no support. Because I'd been a secretary, I had to do my own secretarial stuff. There was no administrative help. I was beginning to feel, 'If you don't watch it, you're going to fall down in a minute.'

I quit and I took my archive with me. It took from '96 to 2001 to convince the City to support it and they have. This is a council building. We've got two rooms here and we've got a record collection down the corridor. They're looking after us. I don't receive any wages. I make a precarious living through gigs, being paid for articles, being paid to do research and consultancy, which comes in now and again I've got very good trustees. They've just about completed putting a bid into the Heritage Lottery Fund, to help keep this place running and hopefully there could be a job in it as well, but I would have to apply for it. We did get lucky at the beginning of the year with Arts Council Wales funding for a part time Jazz Development Worker. Jane, bless her heart, she's absolutely wonderful. She's here two days a week, filling in funding application forms and doing the admin.

This office is our first stage strategy: *Women in Jazz*. We're here to look at what women in jazz in Britain have done and look at what women in Wales in particular have done. We aim to preserve that material, to write it up and promote it through articles and a book. We make sure that the work is preserved for future generations, because if it stops or it's taken away and dispersed, somebody else has to start all over again.

It's one of these feminist sayings that if you don't know your history you've got to start all over again. We're set up here to promote women through education and integration. We work with special needs and we've got close ties with Racial Equality Council, Black History Month. Performance is the part where we either showcase people or one of my bands will host an evening with women in mind, and the fourth segment of it is discovery. The archive part of it, where people can come in and look at the books, look at the journals, listen to something, watch something on video. So that's what we've managed to do up till now.

When I was a lecturer, I decided to do an MSc degree in Women's

Studies, which was an eye opener, as I did not have an O level to my name. It was a two-year taught course and two years then to write up your dissertation. I was writing up my dissertation and I wanted to do it on the history of women in jazz in Britain from 1885. They had great difficulty with this because they couldn't find a tutor to supervise in this field. I found it far easier to find out about American women in jazz than British women. It took me about 18 months to ring round libraries and archives in Britain.' No we haven't got anything and if you find something can you give it to us?'

I started reading books about Jazz in Britain, which were usually written by men about jazz in London. That was basically what they were all about and if they weren't about jazzmen in Britain, they were American books about American men who'd played in Britain. There's an awful lot of them. I started interviewing women and discovered that all sorts of things had been going on. I started making a diary of dates because you're only allowed to use a pencil in reference libraries. I'd scribble like mad, come back, write it up, put it on the computer. I worked that way for two or three years.

The reason why I think women have been left out from our history books in this way, I can only assume that if you're a bloke, and your doing historical research work, and you know that there's no women jazz musicians about, because that's what you know, you're not going to look for them There aren't any, so you're not going to look for any. You write your book about what the blokes did. And then the blokes read it, and more blokes read it, and other generations read it. That's the received wisdom, isn't it? There aren't any because they're not in the books. Finding out all these things has been absolutely incredible. I've been really inspired by it because, for years, from when I had my first gig at 14, you're always told that you're *a one off*, there's nobody else, there haven't been any more, and if there are any, they only sing because they don't play. I accepted it for years because you don't know any better.

I realised that there were all-women bands during the war in America and there were women arrangers and women composers and all sorts of people. I thought this was absolutely brilliant. Looking at the Welsh side of it, it's been absolutely stunning and to think that all this has been going on and nobody else knows about it. It should bloody be known about.

I have to make sure that the *Women in Jazz* project survives, otherwise it all goes down the pan again. Somebody in 2025 might take it in their head, 'I wonder if there were any women playing jazz in Wales?' I think we've gone far too far down the road now for somebody to pull the plug on us. I hope I'm right.

Songstress Update

When I sent Jen's edited transcript to her for comment, she had some great news. The application to the Heritage Lottery Fund has been successful and after applying for the position, she is now working as the Heritage Officer for Women in Jazz. In addition, the organisation has a new Black Heritage project touring schools, funded by the Arts Council for Wales.

Women in Jazz advertising flyer

BEATTIE PUGH

BEATTIE PUGH

Introduction

Patricia Price is a primary school teacher at St. Michael's in Pontypridd. She was leading a Residential Primary Dance Course and I had been invited to work with the children, writing the songs for the production. During our break, Pat told me about her two Aunties, who still sing at family parties, even though they are in their 80's and 90's. She invited me to her 40th birthday party, where I watched Morwen and Beattie, The Two Aunties, do their turn. I was in fits of laughter. It dawned on me afterwards, that I had never seen women of this age performing before and it was a very special evening. We arranged for me to meet Morwen and Beattie, but due to ill health, it wasn't possible. Then, just as my deadlines were about to burn, Pat arranged for me to join her family in visiting Auntie Beattie. Beattie's life could fill a whole book and is such a valuable insight into our local history of song.

When we was young we used to go up to someone's house on a Sunday, and we used to have a concert. We'd give the little ones a saucepan and a spoon or a brush and we'd have a concert. No music... and we used to sing.

We had it in the night-time and it was dark. One night we heard something drop on the ceiling, so me, Morwen and Bessie ran out because we didn't know what was happening. We left all the kids in the house. When we got out there, I said, 'Oh heck, we'd better go and get the kids out!' It was such a bang. I was shaking.

The idea is that we have a go in a concert. We'll always have a go, whether we can sing or not. It was all very close. In and out of each other's houses, the door always open and we'd all help each other out.

Well, there we are, that's us. If anybody went to hospital them days, somebody would knock the door and give a flannel and somebody else would give a bit of soap or lend a towel or a nightdress, or something. That's the way we were down there. We'd help one another all the time. It was that sort of street.

If we wanted entertainment, then we'd all to go up to the top of the mountain.

My mother used to make Welsh cakes, and whiten our daps. We'd take all the Welsh cakes and everything up the mountain with us. And Corky Collins, he had a trombone. Nora's father had an accordion. Snowball had a mouth organ. And we all used to go up that mountain.

We'd stay from about 9 o'clock in the morning until about six in the evening and that was our holiday, singing and dancing all day long.

Singing and dancing was all we had to do, isn't it? We made our own arrangements, our own little concerts. Carrying chairs down Taff Street because we were always having a concert. We used to put a concert on in the Tavern. Dai Price was the comedian, and they used to have us up there. We used to play cricket in the street on a Sunday – no bat, no ball – but we used to play cricket! We used to quarrel and all, if somebody fouled!

It was before the war because I worked then down in Bridgend during the war, down in the ammunition factory. And my money was 7/6d. I'd catch the train, 4 O'clock in the morning. We were working in the black powder. I worked all through the war... and they were trying to bomb the arsenal. They bombed Llantrisant and there was a big crater there. But we all had to go down into the shelter and I wouldn't go because I had a fear of going down in that shelter and getting...   all them people together. I'd always be the last to go down and I'd be more or less sitting just by the entrance. And they'd say, 'Where's Beattie?'

No, I didn't want to go down there, not with all them people. And I was thinking, 'Oh no, if they bombed it...' We just waited until the air raid would go. They'd blow it and then we'd go back to work.

We used to talk down there, some used to take knitting. They used to finish their knitting in there. And they'd be singing down there. We always sang Welsh songs. Or, sometimes we'd sing 'Show me the way to go home...' It used to be good to hear us all singing in there. Yes, you know, we were frightened, but we always seen the funny side of things.

My friend Maureen Davies had a pal there. We were coming off the afternoon shift and he was going in the night shift and he said, 'Is it alright tonight, Beat?' and I said, 'Yes.' And that night he got killed. Blew... Black powder and it exploded, and he got killed. It was happening all the time. We were on detonators, smaller than my fingernail. And if one dropped it, they'd shout. So we had to stay as we were. One woman from Mount Pleasant, she had her foot blown off, because the detonator had gone in her shoe and they were so small, you wouldn't know. We didn't wear our own shoes, we had to wear like big ones, and a jacket, and cover all our hair. No clips, no rings, nothing. And she had a big shoe on see... Well, when she put that shoe on ... bang! It was a frightening experience, but we had to do it and that was it. We had to go to work.

Well, we knew when all the men were coming from the pit because them days, they used to sing coming home, down the street. Always singing. Our Leonard, and Phil, and Frankie O'Brian, all of them would be coming down off the night shift, and they'd be singing coming down the street.

Oh God it was a hard life. Terrible hard life. It was hard times, when you didn't know where the next meal was coming from. When we was young we used to go to funerals and we didn't know who had died, but we'd go to their funerals. And my mother said, 'Take Beattie because it will save a meal.' We'd go for the tea and a sandwich.

I'd say to Bessie, 'Well, who's dead then?'

She'd say, 'Hang on now …'

In those days the coffin used to be in the houses and she'd go across and if it was a woman, Bessie would say, 'Oh, we're distant relatives of hers …'We didn't know the dead woman. We never knew.

Bessie found out if there was a funeral. If it was a man, we'd be a distant relative of him. It was saving my mother a meal. We could last until about Thursday, but after Thursday then there was nothing left in the house. It was hard going then, hard going.

These days they go abroad to get married. And me, I had to stay in the house and do the dishes and go for the meat. And that was 53 years, now, 10th January. And Dick died on the 12th. Our anniversary was on the 10th and he died on the 12th and he got buried on the 15th.

I buried him twelve years ago this month. If you were walking by here now, you'd have to say hello to him first, and then he'd get into conversation. But he wouldn't say anything. He couldn't go in a conversation.

And the way he picked me! I was serving him tea at the afternoon shift. Kitty said, 'He's a nice looking fella.'

'Well,' I said, 'I haven't noticed. And I was afternoon shift and I was serving now, and he come in. 'Can I have a tea?' and I filled the tea and I took the money off him. He went to the door and he turned round and he said, 'Do you like the pictures?'

And I said, 'Yes.'

'Will you meet me by the castle,' he said. 'Saturday night?'

And I said, 'Yes.' And that was it.

'Kitty,' I said, 'Do you know that fella … with the white teeth? I've got a date with him on Saturday.'

'Oh,' she said. 'Don't be dumb. Come with me instead.'

'No,' I said, 'I'll go and see if he turns up.'

Well, I went didn't I and he was there. He bought me sweets but them days in the picture house it was all wooden floors. There weren't carpets then. And he paid 1/9 and that was a dear seat that was. He'd bought me these boxes of sweets, they were like a Malteser, only they were a bit like a nut in them. He went, 'Here you are.'

'Oh, thank you.' So I opened them up and I said, 'Do you want one?' But I opened the wrong end, didn't I, and they all fell out! And on the wooden floor.

He always said, 'I had my warning that day,' he said. 'I took her to the pictures. Why did I do it then?' But he came my way in the end. He had dry sayings. Well, when you catch him, very dry sayings.

We used to go up the Pentrebach Club, and we got friendly there. One week they said, 'There's hypnotism on tonight.'

'Right.'

Then they'd say, 'I want five people to come up, Beattie …?'

Dick said, 'Beattie, Don't you move.'

I said, 'Why?'

'Don't you move now,' he said. Everyone was shouting, 'Come on, Beattie!'

I said to Dick, 'Look, they're calling me up …'

'Never mind, ignore them. Don't you go up.'

'Oh, I've got to go.' And up I'd go. Well, the man hypnotised four people.

They just went straight to sleep but he couldn't do me. He was touching me saying, 'You are asleep. 'You are asleep….'

'No, I'm not,' I'd say. And he tried again.

'Now,' he said. 'You are asleep.'

'Oh well, do you want me to go to sleep?' I said.

When I was on the stage everyone was laughing and I could see Dick. He ended up walking out. He told me, 'Get off,' he said. 'I can't put up with you,' he said. He could not come my way. No way, he couldn't.

At the club then, if anybody could do a turn they could win a Sunday lunch in a basket: potatoes, carrot, cabbage, the winner would have all that. Well, I went up.

I said to the audience, 'I can't sing,' but I was singing. And I won it! I came home with the basket.

Now before I got up to sing, I could see Dick getting up out of his chair to leave and I shouted, 'Stop that man by there now, from going out!'

They said over the microphone, 'Dick, come on back. Come on back and sit.'

He come back, but later he said, 'Now, from now on, you do what you like, but don't ask me in.'

Well, we put a concert down in town, me and Doll from next door, and all the rest of the girls. I said to Dick, 'You want to come to the concert, don't you?'

'Oh, what are you doing?'

'Oh,' I said, 'I'm only singing in the group at the beginning.'

'Are you sure now?'

'Yes, that's all I'm doing,' I said. 'I'm singing in the group.'

'Oh …'

Well, he went with five other husbands and our Leonard and Ceinwen was there. Instead of us coming through the curtain on the stage, we had to come through the club and walk down the aisle. And there we were, [sings and taps] 'My name is Mac Namara, I'm the leader of the...' I had an accordion, and I had big working boots on, trousers, a big, long mac, with all medals. We thought of everything... and I had a Dai cap on. I had the accordion with one strap. Well, it was heavy, wasn't it? But before I went up I'd drunk five vodkas and lemons just to help me along.

Len was sitting there and I come through, see. He said, 'Oh God, look at Beattie …' No, Dick wouldn't turn his head. He said, 'No, she's been on. She's been singing in the group at the beginning.'

Our Len said, 'Well, Dick, who was that then?'

'She told me she was only singing in the group.' He was going down in his seat. He said, 'She told me she was only in the singing.' Well, the next thing I was in the Hawaii sketch. Len said, 'Look Dick.'

'Oh, no,' he said, 'Oh no, not her again.' Then I was in The Supremes. (sings) 'Baby Love, my Baby Love...'

I was doing all of it. I was a ballerina then. I had to pick my mate up – not that I'm saying she were big. In rehearsals she was jumping, but when we were on the 'real McCoy', she wouldn't move. And I said, 'Now look Ann, I'll be walking off,' I said. 'I can't lift you.'

She was in a tutu and I was in leotards. I said, 'Ann, I'm going to walk off if you don't jump.' In the end, she jumped. And I said, 'Well, thank God.'

At the end Dick said, 'Hey Len. Don't miss her now.' He said, 'No, she's doing every bloody thing! She's been in everything,' he said.

When I came home he said, 'Why did you say you were only going to do the singing, when you were doing all that?'

And I said, 'Did you enjoy it?'

'Yes,' he said.

So, there was somebody from Abercaneth who had been watching the show. He was putting a show on up there and he booked us. 'I'm putting on a show,' he said. 'I want to know if these would go?'

Well, he asked the committee. They weren't willing for us to go because they were having more trade with us doing the show down there.

In the end they agreed and we put the shows on down there and on the first night, who was the first dressed to come? Dick, yes, he was there. Ready, dressed ready. And he used to run me and my friend home next door from the club.

After that, we went and we done it for the old age people. We dressed in old-fashioned clothes. I had an umbrella and a big hat. We sold tickets by the door. I think I had fifteen vodkas. I said to Ann, 'Well,' I said, 'we look like paupers, me and you. Look at them all dressed lovely.'

'Ah but,' she said, 'me and you are happier than that lot.'

My mate sent her husband over to tell me and Ann now, 'Tell them not to drink too much because they'll be making a fool of themselves.' In Mac Namara's band! Cheeky devil!

'Oh,' I said, 'Oh, thank you for coming to tell us.' I shouted to my friend's husband, 'John, two vodkas!' I said, 'Yes, two vodkas'. How can you make fools of yourself in Mac Namara's Band?

We done that for the old age for nothing. We didn't charge them nothing!

We all made something, cakes and that. And I'm going back now nearly 40 years, more than 40 years that we done it, down there.

I went and called Bingo up the bingo hall. Went up there, we had a singsong up there last Christmas. Still I'd get up now, if someone asked me.

Beattie, Morwen and friends in Mini Caldwell's Rolls Royce

FRANKIE ARMSTRONG

Extract edited from *As far as the eye can sing*.
An Autobiography by :-

FRANKIE ARMSTRONG

Introduction

Years ago, I was gigging the circuit in Cardiff, when I noticed posters for performances and workshops with the name Frankie Armstrong splashed across them. Her name seemed to be everywhere. It never occurred to me, and why should it, that this well-travelled songstress had a visual impairment, until I read her autobiography.

I really wanted to meet her but trying to get hold of Frankie Armstrong proved almost impossible. I think our answer phones got quite close in the end! Running out of time, we decided that it might be easier for me to take an edited extract approved by Frankie, from her book, As far as the eye can sing.

I was running some workshops for *Graeae Theatre Company*, the only professional company for actors with disabilities, when I heard they were planning a production to tour India. When it was suggested that I join the company for the tour, I juggled eagerly with my diary dates to make room for the rehearsal period. The show was being directed by a young director, Nigel Jamieson, who was excited at the prospect of my joining them. We arranged to meet and hit it off immediately: we have remained friends ever since.

We were a most extraordinary group. I had heard about Nabeil Shaban and found him as electrifying as I had been led to believe. Nabs had brittle bones and is very small and confined to a wheelchair, but the term 'wheelchair-bound' is peculiarly inappropriate to him. He moves his wheelchair with the same expressivity as his face and hands: it is simply an extension of himself. Jag Plah, an Indian with cerebral palsy, is equally extraordinary. Jag has rare charm and exceptional clarity of perception. Eli Wilkie, a beautiful woman with a fine singing voice, had severe muscular dystrophy which meant that she, too, was in a wheelchair, with her by then very curved spine causing her to sit with her face always tilted. In spite of this, she sang like a lark. Jim Gibbon, also small with a severely curved spine, could manage some time out of the wheelchair so long as the activity wasn't too tiring. I had convinced him at a workshop that being small didn't mean he couldn't sing strongly and he turned out to have a great voice.

Our starting point was physical warming-up exercises and improvisations, to give Nigel an idea of what we could do physically. This was my first encounter with the style of work developed by Jacques LeCoq. Out of this emerged wondrous things. Who would ever have imagined a spastic juggling, or doing one of those theatrical falls, flat on the face – or Nabs riding his wheelchair with the whirling, rearing, plunging motions of a Roman charioteer, and me spinning my white cane like a drum majorette? We had a wonderful time testing out all the possibilities, pushing our limitations to their outermost boundaries and finding some images of great theatricality in the process. Nigel trusted us to work within the margins of safety and left us to define what these were: a lesser director would have called a halt long before. We began exploring scenes from our own lives, setting up naturalistic improvisations and finding imagery to express the struggles, frustrations and triumphs that, to some degree, we had all experienced. By week two we began to see a shape emerging. We would tape our improvisations and next morning Nigel would turn up with a scripted version. Then he would say, 'Frankie, could you write us a song for this point in the script before tomorrow?' Somehow I did. We were all being pushed to our limits, yet somehow we got the show together on time.

At last the big day arrived and we settled into our seats on the Air India Jumbo, eating curry and feeling that the pressures had all been worthwhile. In Bombay city we found ourselves booked into a luxury hotel overlooking a beach with palm trees. We visited Calcutta and Delhi and saw many amazing sights. The best part of each visit was the time spent in the special school for spastics, where the quality of the work and of the relationships struck us as soon as we entered the door. The children were, of course, from middle-class homes: we were distressed to see poor spastic children begging in the streets, but this sad fact couldn't detract from the quality of the work we saw in the special schools.

In every city there were receptions with local officials, but we also made sure that we visited the local flea markets. The sight of three small people in metal and chrome wheelchairs, two on shiny crutches and me with my white cane, all looking cheerful and colourfully dressed, literally stopped the traffic. Indians have a different sense of personal space from us: we often found ourselves at a standstill with people, animals and traffic blocking every visible road while we were gently poked, stroked and patted. Once when I was pushing Eli's wheelchair we found ourselves surrounded with kids, all bending down to peer at Eli's beautiful face as she sat in her bent-forward position. I could see neither her expression nor theirs and said to the back of her head, 'Eli, I'd just love to know what expression you have on your face at the moment.' Her reply was, 'A beatific smile!'

Our performance in Delhi was to be at the Nehru Centre. When we arrived at midday for a tech run, armed guards were visible on the roof. It had been rumoured that Mrs Ghandi was planning to attend and the sight of the guards certainly lent credence to the rumours. Halfway through our lighting run, we were interrupted by a security guard with a metal detector who marched up on stage and proceeded to wave his clocking, clacking machine in all directions. 'Click' and 'clack' it well might, as there were two wheelchairs, several crutches, my cane and five prop stands on stage, all made of metal. Nigel, usually good natured to the last, yelled at him to get off stage as we were in mid rehearsal and time was short, but this made no impression on the robotically clicking man and machine, who left in his own time without in any way acknowledging the presence of human beings in his metallic world.

Be it the consequence of nerves or years on diuretics for glaucoma, the last thing I do before any performance is go to the loo. I used our travelling portaloo behind a screen backstage, took my place behind the curtain and closed my eyes to begin the centring process I needed before curtain up. Disconcertingly, I realized that the bottoms of my trousers were soaking wet. It then dawned on me that someone must have removed the plastic bag from the portaloo and I had peed all over my trouser bottoms and feet. I was recovering from this ignominious realization when I heard feet shuffle towards me from the wing. A voice whispered, 'The Prime Minister has arrived. Oh, the Prime Minister has arrived. I thought you would all be pleased to know!' And the feet shuffled back into the wings.

The curtain went up and I launched into song, for the first time before a Head of State, peed-on feet and all. After the performance Mrs Ghandi came backstage, dressed very simply in a grey sari. She had serenity about her and her manner was direct and warm. It was hard to realize that she was also, inevitably, a scheming and ambitious woman. I found myself profoundly shocked when I heard a year later that she had been killed.

LYNNE GENT

LYNNE GENT

Introduction

At the suggestion of Pat Smith, I contacted Lynne Gent from Pontardawe. I telephoned her and visited her in her home. I think she was quite taken aback at how much she has actually contributed to song throughout her life. Sometimes, it isn't until you sit down and tell someone else what you have been doing over the years, that you realise the extent of your work. Lynne's incidental meeting on a train with a woman carrying a banjo introduced her to a lifetime interlaced with folk music.

In 1966 I came down to Wales from Morecambe to Swansea University and there was a girl on the train. She was carrying this big black box. A funny, black box. I thought, 'Strange black box.' I'd never seen one of those before. Anyway, turned out to be a banjo. We were both on the same floor in college in the first year. She was the person who introduced me to songs which had a real story. They gave you history and they told you what it was like in those days, and that's what I enjoyed, the fact that there was a story that you could tell. We started singing together and by the end of that year we'd got so involved in the University Folk Club, we were virtually running it. The following year, we were booking artists mostly over the border in England. I'm not sure when I started picking up on Welsh artists, it was probably a while before I did that...

I also used to go to the old Adelphi Club, in Wine Street, Swansea. The Adelphi ran a sort of folk club, but it did a lot of Blues as well. Eventually as a female singer, unaccompanied, I started looking further afield and found the Pontardawe Club, which had been going for 2 years. It's been going about 33 years now. *Ruth Stevenson* was singing at the club, so we became good friends. In fact, I'm her daughter's godmother. We sang together at odd times. We started just the two of us, calling ourselves *Strumpet*. Then we were approached to form a new version of the band, *Swansea Jack*. We got together as a foursome, because we'd all actually been in the band, messing around in the very early days of *Swansea Jack*. We went over to Spain to tour and while we were over there, the guy who ran Guimbarda Records was really taken with the dress I was wearing. It was an Indian dress and it had a piece of embroidery set into it .He really fancied this piece of embroidery so took a photograph of it and he used it as the cover for the LP he released. It was an LP of John and Sue Kirkpatrick. John Kirkpatrick is the top diatonic accordion player, I would say in Britain, and at the time, was performing with his wife. So my little piece of dress is on the front cover of John Kirkpatrick's LP in Spain, entitled *Threads and Patches*.

About four years ago, I got a really bad bout of bronchitis and I was off work for four months. I didn't sing for another a year. I didn't have much of a voice for yet another year, and then it's gradually come back, slowly. It's taken nearly four years.

The Pontardawe festival came out of the Folk Club, but also involved people interested in the community and not the music. The Folk Club itself did the rounds of the pubs in Pontardawe. I think it's been in every pub, some more than once.

It started off in *The Cross* which used to be a hotel, probably the first hotel in Pontardawe, but that had closed down. There was just a coffee bar there, which is why people like Ruth could go along, because she was underage for drinking at the time, whereas I was old enough, when I joined two years later. The guy who'd started the Folk Club, Brian Harris, well, he was there in the very early stages, ran it for a long time. Sadly, after several years as the mainstay of the club, he had a brain tumour, and died. He'd always wanted to start a festival in Pontardawe, so that inspired us to do it.

There was a steel works here that closed down in the early 60's. Eventually it had been all cleared, and it was just derelict land, behind the shops, so we actually organised the festival there. It consisted of 2 marquees joined together with a corridor and a little marquee in the middle, which was the bar. That's all it was. We had a concert in one and ceilidh in the other and it was brilliant. People camped on the side. I always remember the budget being about fourteen thousand pounds and in 1978 that was a lot of money. You know, you think, 'My god how did we have the confidence to go and do that,' but it was what we wanted to do, so we did it.

For the first 11 years of the festival's life, I had a major role of some sort. I was chairman. I did the bookings for 3 years; I did the publicity, designed posters, badges all sorts of things. ... then I had a break, then went back into it in a small way, doing all the backdrops for the stages.

The problem was, I decided to go into teaching. I've had all sorts of bits and bobs of jobs, but I'd been to Art College and I was doing ceramics. I set up a studio down in *The Cross* in the basement, and I was doing evening classes but I thought, 'I'm not getting anywhere with this.' I really enjoyed teaching adults, so I went and did a B.Ed in Maths, which is my subject. There wasn't anything going in Art but they were desperate for Maths teachers. That killed my social life stone dead. If I'd been a youngster going into teaching, I probably would have spent 3 or 4 years, got it together and I'd have been all right. All the semi-professional singers I used to meet around the club, so many of them were teachers. I reckon they all taught in primary school because I tell you what, going into Comprehensive School at 46, I was absolutely shattered.

I wished I'd learnt to play an instrument, which I never did, because I spent a lot of time in the early days really concentrating on singing. There seemed to be two schools of thought in traditional song. You either performed your song or you did it dead straight and let the words tell the story itself. I was more a performer and liked to put like passion or feeling into it and so used to spend a lot of time practising: meaning all the time to learn to play guitar or a keyboard, but whatever time I had spare went on my singing. I have got a decorative style. Infact, one of the guys in *The Chieftains* said, ' You sing like the pibroch, there's got to be Irish in you. You're the spitting image of my cousin's daughter.' And of course there is quite a lot of Irish in me. Both my parents are from Irish stock, so I felt chuffed. I had a good voice and I had lots of compliments. But I think you have to have the courage to go out and do it. You have to have the push. I can think of people who haven't got half the talent of several people I know, but because they've got the drive to go and do it, they've done it, they've improved, and they're doing fine. I'm sort of jack-of-all-trades, master of none when it comes down to doing things. I've got interests in all sorts of things but I've only really tinkered with any of them.

If I'd have been a man…they seem to have more confidence. As far as the tradition goes, a man can sing a quiet romantic song and they can sing all sorts of sea songs, rowdy songs, funny songs, jolly songs. It's easier to sing those, even if you don't play an instrument. It's a lot easier to do a bigger range of songs and feel as if you could do a whole evening and keep people interested…

My dream was to be a full time singer. I would have loved to have done it. My father had the same dream and he didn't follow his dream. He sang like Paul Robeson. He worked in a factory and they used to stop the machines to listen to him. so I think I got my voice from him, I suppose it's always been a little bit of me.

RUTH EXELL STEVENSON

Edited from a personal history written by: -

RUTH EXELL STEVENSON

Introduction

My first ever festival performance was in the Club Tent at Pontardawe. I didn't meet Ruth at the festival, but I knew she was the Artistic Director. It seemed to me that anyone who was anyone knew Ruth. Many years later, here I was planning to interview her and my nerves were getting the better of me! I really wanted to make a good impression, so I dumped the jeans and went for a skirt. Mistake! It was a cold icy night. I pulled up on the hill outside her cottage. It was so icy that on getting out of the car, I fell over! So much for the skirt! Nursing my grazed knees, with blood trickling slowly down my tights, I tried to look composed. She opened the door and was faced with me, biting back the tears, trying to pretend it was fine. She was so lovely, so kind and caring as she welcomed me into her beautiful home. While we were cleaning up my knees, I explained how nervous I had been. Ruth said that she had been anxious too, waiting for Cheryl Beer to arrive. We laughed about it and had a great evening chatting, looking at her amazing collection of photographs and memorabilia. Seems something of an extreme way of breaking the ice, literally and metaphorically!

It was at Pontardawe Grammar School that I started to learn the harp and violin. I soon decided that catgut sounded better plucked than bowed, and plumped for the harp – the bonus was it got me out of Latin lessons once a week! By this time I'd started to teach myself guitar. I had a huge Framus Black Rose guitar, which was almost as big as me! A few of us third formers met up with some of the sixth form boys, got ourselves invited to a barbecue that evening and ended up singing round the inevitable camp fire. Mary Hopkins was one of the sixth formers and she was one of the founders of the new Valley Folk Club in Pontardawe. Anyway, they persuaded a few of us to start going to the folk club, which was where I met Brian and Mary Harris, two teachers who were the mainstay of the club. Brian and Mary came to see my parents to persuade them to let me carry on going to the club after it moved to the Dynevor Arms; a pub with none too good a reputation!

Dr Thomas, my harp teacher, found out I was interested in folk music and decided to buy a Celtic harp for the school. Well, for me really, since no-one else played it at first. I used to play at Eisteddfodau, church, school and guide concerts. Meanwhile, along came 'O' and 'A' Levels, which I have to admit I didn't exactly shine at – mainly because I got myself so interested in folk music and would spend hours copying out and learning songs instead of learning riveting stuff like the periodic tables and translating the Punic Wars. After 'A' Levels I did a secretarial course at Neath Technical College and went off to London in 1971 to seek my fortune! London was great .The folk clubs there were really popular and had loads of great floor singers, most of whom were booked at other festivals in Britain. I sang a few times but then I discovered rock music and started singing with a band .The least said the better, though we did make money! After a while I decided I couldn't stand the City and lack of mountains any more and came home to the much clearer air of Swansea.

When I got back from London, I rented a room in a house belonging to Mick and Alison Themes. Mick was a journalist from Ilford who had moved to Wales to work on the South Wales Evening Post and both he and Alison were interested in folk music. I also met up with Mike James and Katie Vavantakis at the university folk club and eventually formed the first incarnation of Swansea Jack. We were moderately successful and got a fair number of gigs. Mick moved away to Llantrisant and Katie went off to marry Carter in Vermont. Mike and I continued to help run the folk club. We sang together and were joined by Lynne Gent, a singer I'd admired for years since I first heard her sing back in 1969. Eventually we teamed up as a duo called Strumpet. Joined by other musicians, it transpired that at some time or other we had all played in Swansea Jack, thus, we re-named ourselves.

Guimbarda Records in Spain, who had bought the rights to the Swansea Jack album, contacted us and they asked would we like to go on a week-long tour of Spain in June with other bands. Would we ever! We were flown to Madrid and treated like superstars, with champagne receptions and full suites each at the hotels we stayed in. We opened the first gig at the Casa De Campo in Madrid to some 60,000 people. It was so hot, 106 in the shade, that my harp strings were going up and down in pitch as I played. As I walked on stage, I was greeted by thousands of people yelling, 'El harpa, El harpa' – what a buzz! After we got off stage we were met by the organiser of a festival in Gallicia, who booked us on the spot. We'd be playing alongside Milladoro, one of Spain's most respected bands and one of my favourite bands at the time. We went onto Valencia where everything fell apart. Apparently at the gig in

Malaga, the people waiting to get inside decided to storm the gates, so no one paid. The tour organisers lost a lot of money and by the time we got to Valencia the sound crew decided to pull out at the last minute. Luckily we had return air tickets. This didn't put us off and the festival in Ortiguera de Santa Maria was great. We played a few gigs after that but with Mike moving to Brittany and Lynne now living in Carmarthen, the band couldn't really keep going. I had started to go down to Llanrhidian on the Gower, to music evenings at the Britannia Inn, or The Brit as we all called it. It was here that I met Peter Blainey, a past All Ireland Champion, and he taught me how to play the bodrhan. His niece, Trisha, had a summer job as a barmaid. Trisha and I got on really well and the following year I went over to Ireland to stay with her at her flat, the infamous 'Blue Door', in Dundalk. It was amazing. I met so many musicians and singers, learnt so many songs, and made so many friends. It's hardly surprising I ended up with a huge repertoire of Irish songs.

The folk scene in South Wales was thriving at that time and there were so many folk clubs that the circuit was very busy if erratic. A group of like-minded folk club organisers got together and formed the South Wales Folk Federation (SWaFF). The idea behind it was to rationalise tours and make it easier for clubs to get popular acts down more often. It was through SWaFF that I got to know Geoff Cripps, Linda Simmonds, Steve Reikoff, Gil and Jenny Kilbride (parents of the Kilbride Brothers), Mike Harber, Derek and Sara Smith, Ned Clamp, Rory Furlong and others, all of whom were to help with the formation of the first Pontardawe Festival. A group of us from the folk club had been talking for ages about putting on a festival. Part of the reason was that at that time none of the 'big' folk acts came west of Cardiff. This was pre-M4, so we thought it was time they started playing down this end of Wales. One afternoon, we were talking about a festival in the bar of the Dynevor Arms, when the landlord put £20 down on the table and said, 'Stop talking about it and do it!' The result was the Pontardawe Celtic Music Festival, which was held in August of 1978. I was asked to become the publicity officer along with Dave Haines, that was the start of a major part of my life and became something of an obsession with me. Ask anyone who knows me!

In 1980, I married Ian Stevenson, an Irish musician, then living in Derry, Northern Ireland, and we went on to form Will Griffy's Music with John Howes and John Morgan. Our daughter Isobel was born on 16th December 1982, and one of my favourite memories is standing at the front window of my mother's house on Christmas Eve, with Isobel in my arms being serenaded by the Folk Club carollers. New Year's Eve was fairly memorable too – being jammed in between an Irish piper and a box player, with Isobel fast asleep in my arms in the sitting room of our cottage! She's always loved music, especially the pipes, and is a good singer herself, though, like me, prefers the organisational side of the music nowadays.

Then we had our son, Jamie, and with babies and work, my singing and playing waned somewhat. I took a back seat, doing bookings for the band and, of course, the Festival.

It had become very international by this time and the days of one marquee and a beer tent were long gone. The organisation of the event was huge and it became practically a full-time occupation for most of the people involved. We were, as we are now, a completely voluntary organisation – the only people who got paid were the artists and the hire companies. Even my mother was roped in – she ran the Flower Festival.

I split up with my husband in September 1992. The Festival and my music helped me to come to terms with being a working, single mother. I had been left with huge debts and after a period of ill health, I had what amounted to a breakdown. I retired from the Fire Service after 20 years service. When I finally 'got my head together' I realised what a mess my finances were in, and that I had nearly lost our home. I ended up doing a series of low-paid jobs, anything to keep the mortgage paid and bread on the table. The friends I had made through Festival, along with my mother, were a huge support and helped to put me back on track.

By 1995 the festival had grown to such an extent we couldn't run it from our homes any more and we set about trying to get a proper office. We'd had a desk in the reception office at the Cross Community Centre for some years but we had, by this time, got a part-time administrator and we really needed somewhere of our own. There was a semi-derelict pub, the Pontardawe Inn, which had been closed for two years and was up for sale, where we'd always run festival fundraisers and sessions. With help from a grant from the Foundation for Sports and Arts and Buckley's Brewery, we managed to raise the money to buy it, but were faced with a major renovation job. Everyone pitched in and for six long weeks we hacked off plaster and rendering, fitted plasterboard, re-plastered, filled loads of skips with rubble, stripped wood, put in new floors, piping, cables, built a bar, painted and laboured mightily until on 5th May we were officially opened for business by the Festival Patron, Peter Hain MP.

The reaction from the press was fantastic. We got a full page in The Independent and were even featured on 'Country File.' The pub was packed out every weekend and we were lucky enough to be able to put on lots of great bands regularly. If a band happened to be touring in the area and had a free night, they'd come along and play. Not bad for a little village pub in Wales. By 2000 I'd roped my daughter into helping to organise part of the Festival. She won a Millennium Award to put on a series of concerts aimed at showcasing local young bands. She did this very successfully.

A run of bad weather at Festival for a few years followed by the foot and mouth epidemic in 2001 forced us to cancel that year's Festival and led to us having to sell the pub, though we did keep the office on a lease from the new owners. That year was very strange. The town council and local licensees realised how much the Festival brought to the village and decided to run a scaled down Village Festival, which I was asked to get involved with.

I became an adviser to many different festivals. Meanwhile in Pontardawe, hopes of a return to the field festival were dashed due to lack of money. We moved into the Arts Centre for 2002 and 2003 but everyone missed the atmosphere of being on the field. Luckily, things started to look brighter on the financial front and we successfully moved back to our traditional field venue at Parc Ynysderw in 2004. 2005 sees the festival still in Parc Ynysderw.

Thanks to encouragement from many sources, not least Cheryl Beer's Heaven Scent: The History of the Welsh Songstress, I've now re-strung my harp and started re-learning songs and tunes. So, who knows, perhaps Lynne Gent and I will get together again and revive the old duo. Should be fun!

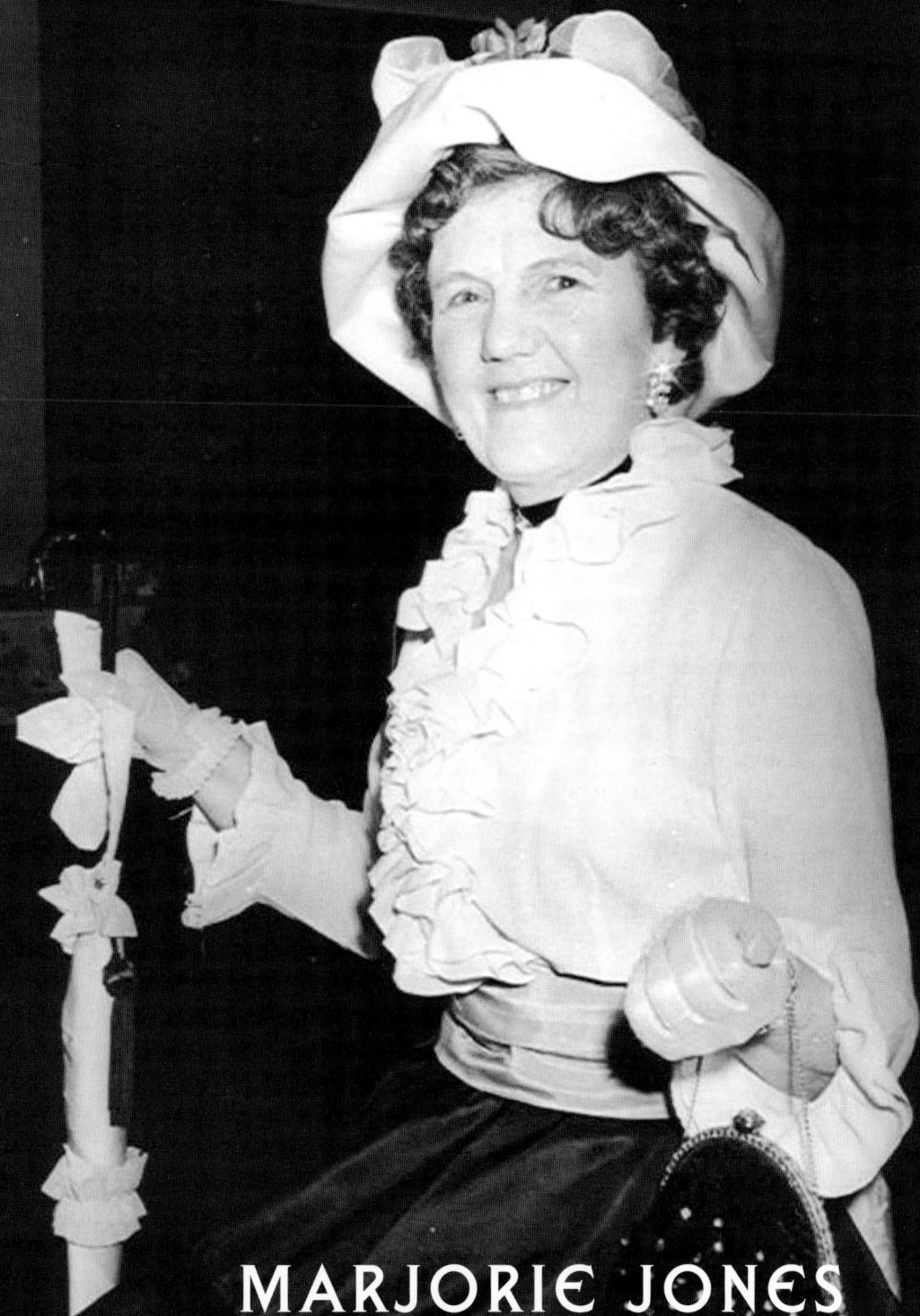

MARJORIE JONES

MARJORIE JONES

Introduction

Marjorie Jones is the mother of Heather Jones. Still very much immersed in song, she gives us an insight into the Town's Women's Guild and the impact that such organisations had on women's social lives. Marjorie's experience of song is one of togetherness and community, with a group of women that have not just shared music and drama but consequently their whole lives.

My father was a singer but unfortunately he died when I was eleven, so all I know, really stemmed from that. I never played an instrument at all, because having lost my mother at four, We didn't have lessons or anything. We couldn't afford to. We didn't have piano lessons or anything like that.

I joined this ladies' choir in 1955 to have one night out a week somewhere, because there wasn't much going. That's why I joined the Towns Women's Guild because that gave you speakers and all sorts of things. We've done lots of shows. It was wonderful, but of course now they don't want that anymore. That's why the TG and WI are losing quite a lot of members ...well they're just OAP's at TG now. My daughter never joined it, she wouldn't want to join it. It seems to be for the older people. Because we're getting older and older, we are either going into nursing homes or dying.

Back in the 50's we were hardly supposed to go out, we were supposed to mind the children. I had three. The TG was my night out once a week. My husband worked hard. He was a representative for a firm and he was always writing up orders in the evening, so I suppose it was difficult in a way. I couldn't have joined a band. I couldn't have done that. I couldn't leave the children. I had three children, two boys and a girl. Heather was the youngest. I don't speak Welsh, but I can read it and I know little bits of it. Very little, not like my daughter, she has learnt it properly and she speaks it properly.

I couldn't do anything during the war. I was in Canada for two years, my husband was over there in the Air Force. He was stationed there for three years and because of that, we were allowed to go out. I took my baby, which was Malcolm then, in 1942 and I came back in 1944. We were fourteen days on the water going and twenty-one days on the water coming back. It's so quick now to get there, but it was quite hard really. We had lifeboat drill twice a day and we had to wear these jackets. We would have these noises on deck, ' All hands on deck, lower the lifeboats.' We didn't know if any of this was real and we had to dash up on deck with the children and line up. They would lower the lifeboats. We were supposed to do that twice a day and I got fed up in the end and I missed quite a few.

It wasn't until 1955 that I joined anything musical. I just loved singing especially part singing. In this ladies' group, we used to sing in three parts and then when I went to the mixed choir it was four parts with the men. Soprano, alto, tenor and bass. I was a mix of soprano, but I sing alto because they always want you more than the soprano. I can still sing it, I am still in a choir and we have just done a work about a fortnight ago, in the University Hall with Carl Jenkins. That was fantastic. He writes some lovely stuff. Our conductor was very good, Alan Guy, he's been going for years and years now. We also have the Town's Women's Musical Festival, and I went once to Brighton. I sang a Welsh folk song unaccompanied and I came second. I was excited. I've done some daft things in my time, some funny things as well, like the Old Bazaar of Cairo. I performed it with a big lady because she's huge and I was so small; we thought it would make it funnier.

I love performing but I also wrote a pantomime for the Towns Women's Guild. I wrote the programme for it as well. That was quite some time ago. We had great fun. The Town's Women's Guild, the TG, is all over the country, more so in England than Wales. It's for people in the town you see, rather than in the country, like the Women's Institute.

We had quite a few girls in Cardiff. We have a Federation called the South Wales Federation. I think we have about sixteen to eighteen girls in it now, but we used to have a lot more. We were ninety-nine members and we are now fifteen. All women. I suppose not long after the war, women wanted to get out and enjoy something, probably because they did have a hard time during the war. I mean, lots were killed just like the men, weren't they?

We had an aunt and two children who were killed in Cardiff in Agincourt Road when a bomb fell through the house. I often think about her. They forget about that, don't they? When you think about the fallen, you don't think about the women who died unnecessarily.

Not every Guild has got a music group. I have got my oldest group, which is only six women now, and I go to the Federation Towns Women's Guilds choir and the Philharmonic Caerdydd in Welsh, but as the years are going on now, I think I am getting a bit past it really. I shouldn't be going, but they pick me up and take me so I go. We are more friends now than anything. Over the years, we have raised a lot for charities. But now we say that we are the charity ourselves, because we are so few. We performed to different groups and different places, mostly in Cardiff, because we had to carry all the stuff around with us, all the props.

There is a lovely school here, its called Ton- yr- Ywen. It's got a lovely stage and lovely curtains. We helped make them actually. We performed there but that lady has died and that lady has died, that's why we have only got six left. One woman was over ninety and she was still playing, she died a couple of years ago.

I always wanted to be in a Gilbert & Sullivan, because we had done it in school, and just when it came to the time to do it, I had scarlet fever, so I wasn't there. I have always had a yearning to do it so I joined a group and I did do it.

I was usually a man because nobody else wanted to wear trousers and dress up as a man. We did *Pretty Little Polly Perkins at Paddington Green*. Well, someone else was Polly Perkins and I was the milkman. We did that loads of times. We loved that one, it was quite funny.

At one of our National Meetings, I managed to speak at the Albert Hall, about one of the things we were discussing, only three minutes mind, and the light would go and you would have to shut up when it went off. It was the highlight of my career. It was absolutely full, the Royal Albert Hall. Well I can't believe I did it now. I was younger then, I don't think I could do it now. It was in the seventies, I think. I went running around that place at the back, to find a way to get on the stage. It was quite difficult. I opened one door and I would have been coming up through the middle.

When I look at photographs of us all performing I think to myself, ' She's died and she's died… She left because she was having an operation on her hip or something.'

I made a lot of the scenery in the garage. We were doing something for Mary Poppins, so I did St Paul's with the clock and everything. It's still in the garage now, but it's filthy dirty. We use to be full of life then.

It was very different being in the mixed choir because you've got the men there, just different really. It's a lovely sound. I like both mind. When it's all women together there's more friendliness. If you asked me the names of some of the men in the mixed choir, I wouldn't know who they were because there were so many. You cant remember them all.

Some of those men, of course, have died. I remember my friend always sat next to me in the mixed choir but she's died; such a lot of people have died. That's how life goes, you've got to accept it all.

My group has had a secret ballot to see if we will continue now there's only 6 of us. We would be very sorry for it to fold, the music particularly. We think, perhaps we'll carry on anyway, even if the Guild finished. We could just keep the choir going. I found a lady who plays the piano and she has replaced our original pianist who died. I sang solos, but I mean, I'm an amateur, absolutely, and I don't profess to be anything else. Sometimes we would have expenses; people were very kind. They would say, 'Oh yes, we must give you something.' It's only to buy your music, because music is quite expensive you know. It used to be very cheap at one time. I've got lots of music here. I don't know what I am going to do with it. My daughter will have to get rid of it for me. Of course, they photocopy a lot now and they are not supposed to really, it's copyright.

We perform in the OAP places and they are mostly women. We go to one in Birch Grove, Cardiff. They have got a few men and we used to go to one in Ty Celyn just near here and they had a few men, but it's the majority of women who live longer. When we put on the shows, they are awfully kind. They really appreciate it I think.

It's funny because it is only the females in our family that seem to want to sing; my sons don't sing. My sister used to, but father did, you see and he was a man. I don't know if there are any of my grandchildren that want to sing particularly. My Granddaughter does; she sings and they have a little group. My husband used to go out in the morning and come back in the evening and would say, 'You are still singing,' like I've been singing all day. We've always loved it, so there we are.

Without music it would have been a very dull life, I am sure it would. I did enjoy the drama and the acting as well and I've been stage manager in a few of them.

I've spent such a lot of my life singing, more so since my husband died. He wasn't keen on me going out and about much then, but of course it's twenty-six years since he died, so it's a long time. He loved singing. He loved Opera, the good stuff. I'm still busy. Tomorrow I'm going to the practice of the Town's Women's Guild Ladies' Choir and then I'm going to one in the evening as well. I have been very lucky.

ELDRA JARMAN

By kind permission of her daughter, Teleri Gray

TELERI GRAY
Daughter of Eldra Jarman

Introduction

One of the most amazing instruments, that you just have to listen to when you come to Wales, is the Welsh harp. It can move you to tears or smiles in just a matter of notes. I remember one Christmas, I watched a film on S4C about Romany Welsh Harpist, Eldra Jarman, who has now sadly passed away. When I interviewed Heather Jones, it transpired that she had been married to Geraint Jarman. She suggested to me that I should contact Eldra's daughter, Teleri Gray, and talk to her about her mother's life.

Teleri's home is full of wonderful arts and crafts that she has made herself or collected from artists, friends or from one of the many workshops that she has facilitated. She is a charismatic, natural storyteller who captivates. I was enchanted by her warmth and spirituality. With a twinkle in her eye, I knew straight away that she'd be good fun.

When I was little, I remember going to bed and my mother used to play all the music on the harp. I used to fall asleep to it. I can also remember them going out, my Mum and Dad, to here, there and everywhere. They didn't have a car; they couldn't drive, so somebody would always pick them up. And she'd wrap the harp up in a grey blanket, you know those old-fashioned grey blankets, because you have to be careful with them, there's a problem with damp and all that.

I've met loads of people who went to the concerts and who said, 'Oh, your mother was such a beautiful player, and she was such a beautiful woman and I really fancied her...but your father was always there!' It's nice... but I never went. I was a child when she was going out and about doing things, but I do remember another time. There was a place in Aberystwyth. It was called *Pantycelyn* and it was a hotel.

I think it's still there, but it belonged to the Urdd, the Welsh League of Youth, and they'd bought it for Welsh-speaking cultural families to go and meet, like a holiday camp. And of course, there must have been harps there. We used to go there on the train. We went for quite a few summers. In the evening, of course, the kids would be upstairs having pillow fights, or whatever, and then they'd have like a get together and my Mum used to play the harp there. So we were always peeping in. I must have been about twelve, or maybe I was younger than that. It's a long time ago because I'm fifty-nine now. It must have been in the fifties.

I know another story my Mum told me, when she was living in Bethesda, she was an extremely attractive woman, and she must have been playing in an Eisteddfod, and Gypsy Petulengro, he had a group of harpists and dancers in London. He went to Bethesda. And I remember she must only have been about sixteen or something like that and he asked my grandmother, 'Oh please could we have Eldra in our troop?'

'Oh no,' she said. She wasn't going to let her... Too dangerous! Go away! So she wasn't allowed, even though my grandmother was Romany, she still wouldn't let her go with this one to London. 'No! Too dangerous!' So she never went there.

But she did play... she won an Eisteddfod. She couldn't read music, so everything that she played on the harp was taught to her by her father. And everything that he played was taught to him by his father and so on and so forth. My great-great grandfather, and all his sons, played the harp to Queen Victoria and her subjects.

The Romany people passed the harp on from father to son, from father to son. But then my grandfather passed it on to his daughter. He did have sons, but they went off to war. Jack, the eldest... we don't know what happened to him ... he might have taught him but there's no record of it. There were three brothers. All of them were much older than my mother, and the one went off to be a lumberjack in Canada and was never heard of again... Well, he was heard of, he ended up in China somewhere. And then there was another one who was killed in the war, and then there was another one who had shellshock in the war and ended up in a mental hospital. And then there was my mother.

Well, to start it all from the beginning... John Roberts, my great-great grandfather. He was in the *Cambrian Minstrels* and his father was a Welshman called John Robert Lewis. He had 9 sons and a daughter. Can you imagine? And they all lived in a house in the winter and travelled about in the summer. They say that my family were the first people to bring the violin into Wales. *The Roberts Harpists* performed in The Pale

Hall in Bala for Queen Victoria when she came to Wales. I've actually been into the room where they played. It's weird, yes. His wife, the mother, she's there with them but she didn't play anything. She wasn't allowed. She used to bring up the children.

My Great Grandmother's brother, Matthew, now he was very famous. They used to call him *The Badger* or *The Fox* because he used to go off in the winter and live in the hills. My great-grandfather after his wife died, he re-married and they used to play on the promenade in Rhyl together. I think that was about 1913. Without telling his wife, he was stuffing the harp with money, so when he died it was stuffed full of money for her, to look after her. And then my great-cousin, who is about ninety, he used to play with them and they bought him a velvet suit and a velvet cap and he had to go round with the cap. I've spoken to him on the phone and I'm thinking, I can't believe this. Anyhow... it's such a big family you see. It was all men that did all that. But, of course, all this is my mother's background.

I have a portrait of my mother. She was walking down the street one day and this art student saw her and she stopped her and she said, 'Oh you've got such a wonderful face, can I paint you for my course?' So, she does a colour oil painting. My sister still has the original of it and I have a copy.

I didn't really experience discrimination as a child because, of course you see, my father was a professor and so I was always referred to as *Professor Jarman's daughter*. My son is talented. He plays the harp. My mother taught him a bit. But then he went to school and he was taught there... My mother had lent a harp to a girl called Siwan. Then, when my son wanted to learn, Siwan wanted to teach him, to pay back my mother for helping her. So she came to the house and taught him and I gave her a bottle of wine every time she come to the house. It was good.

You see, not many people realize... my family were like *The Rolling Stones* in their day, because they used to travel all around Wales, going from one farm to the other, making music, everybody used to dance, tell stories. And then they'd go to the next farm and tell them about that farm and that was the communication in those days. I mean there was no phone, there was nothing. They were so famous they played to Queen Victoria, they played to this Duke and that Duke and blah de blah... and they were resident harpists in these big houses and everything.

This is one of my favourite stories about our family. My great-great-grandfather and my great-great-uncles, and all the women, decided that it was a bit rough prancing around the country in the winter as well as the summer, so they used to rent houses in the winter. As the cuckoo called, they'd be off. They used to go round the same villages and farms that they've been the year before and they were getting on very friendly with all the farmers. They would take tents with them, or they'd make their own tents – not like tents we've got – they'd make their bender tents. But some of the farmers would let them stay in the barns. And it was warmer in them and of course, they could then play their music, and all the local people would come round and they'd have a barn dance. The farmers would provide the beer and then the harp would be going a bit faster as the beer went down. They all would've thoroughly enjoyed themselves. So that was one way that they sustained themselves and earned a living.

And then another trick of theirs' was... well, this happened by accident really. In one farm what happened was, they were given supper by the farmer and as they were sitting there eating it, the father would say a little prayer in Romany

'And thank you to God for this food that we are provided for by our friends...'

Then they'd eat their food. And when they'd finished their food of course they would always have story telling. Somebody says, 'Oh I've got a story to tell...' But because they were speaking in Romany, the farmer's family didn't know what they were saying. The story telling would go on and on... But then of course the farmers would think that they were still praying. And they could hear them praying and praying and praying all night long.

The farmer came out the next morning after they had been story telling for about three hours in the night, and he and his family thought they were praying for the farm. They'd stayed awake all night listening, but of course they didn't understand a word. They said to my family, 'Well, come up to the house now and we'll make you breakfast...' and my family couldn't understand why. They thought they must have done something wrong.

'Oh, what have you done? Have you been stealing eggs?' they said to the little boy. And he said, 'No, no, no!' Then the farmer explained that they wanted to share breakfast with them because they could hear that they had been praying all night and they wanted to join in, because it was wonderful to have people praying on their land. My family thought that was great! After they'd had a full day's breakfast, they'd think, 'Now what can we do to help you now?' And the farmer would say, 'Well, we've got a lot of rats around,' The gypsies would say, 'Well, we've got ferrets, they're our little pets and they sleep in our pockets. They help us to catch the rats.' So, the farmer would say, 'Right, well this is the haystack...I'll show you where I've seen lots and lots of rats.'

So, they'd all go up and they'd get a stick each and then they'd go looking for rats. Then, when they found them, they'd catch 'em and bash 'em on the head and when the farmer wasn't looking, they'd pick up some of these dead ones and put them in their pockets, because they had big poaching pockets on the outside, and on the inside. The farmer would be very, very pleased. 'Oh thank you very much. You've killed so many of these rats – wonderful.' He'd give them some money. And then he'd say, 'Well, perhaps my friend up the road, he might like to have you up there. You could help him to kill rats...' and they'd think, 'Oh yes, yes, we'll do anything to help anybody. Help us on our way and make some money...'

So, off they'd go to the friend's house up the road and they'd say, 'Now your friend down there, he said you'd like us to come and kill your rats. We've just killed some of his.'

'Oh yes, let me show you where they are.'

And off they'd go and they'd take their sticks with them and they'd start banging around making an even bigger noise, and they might kill a few, but then they'd start pulling out of their poacher's pockets, the other rats that were dead from the last farm, and put them on the floor. They'd be making a big noise... and then the farmer would think, 'Oh, these gypsies are working hard.' He'd say, 'Oh, you've killed all these rats. Oh, thank you very much.' And he'd pay them and then they'd go off laughing to themselves. 'Tee hee...hee...hee... we done a good morning's work today.' I mean they did help, and they did kill rats, but if they could get away with not doing the full whack, then why not, isn't it? And they'd have a good laugh about it.

Eldra Jarman

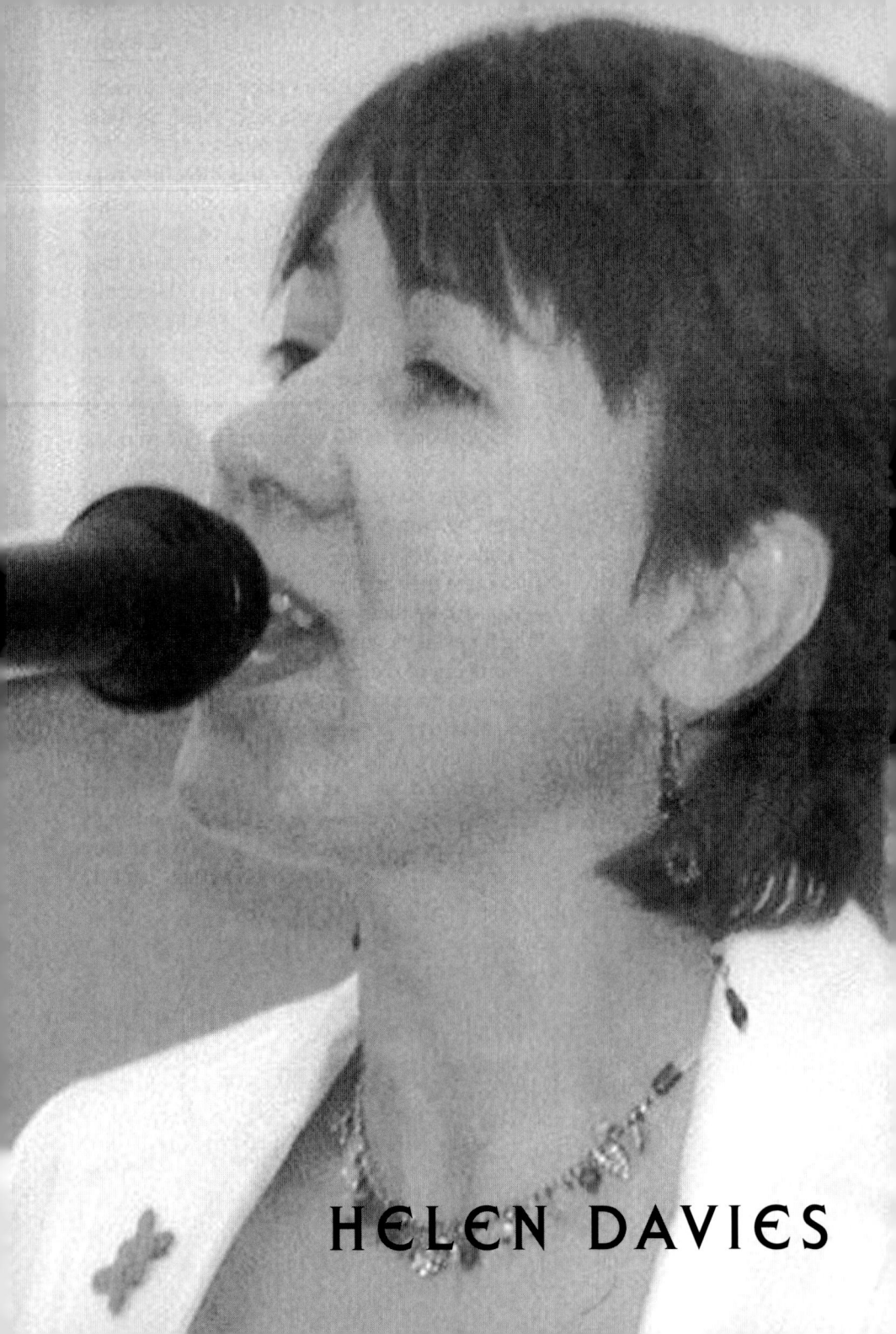

HELEN DAVIES

HELEN DAVIES

Introduction

Helen and I have been song soul mates since we met on a TV programme some years back. She is a human dynamo. A self-motivated, hard working, against-all-the-odds-you-won't-stop-me dynamo! I completely admire her determination. She seems stunned by her own success as a singer, songwriter and more recently as an author. A mulit-gifted wordsmith, Helen is able to move you in just one sentence. A tiny, pint-sized inspiration, with the biggest heart.

My Dad played the bass and the violin and he played in dance bands and the orchestra and things. So I used to sing with my Dad's band as a child. We did old age people's homes and Christmas do's and things like that. So I sang from about the age of three. Dad was into a lot of jazz, so I was singing everything from Nat King Cole, Bing Crosby and Helen Shapiro, as a child.

I was born in 1957, so I would say I started singing when I was about... in about 1960. Well, my mother tells stories... my Auntie Eileen used to work in the Co-op in Cannock. She worked in the drapery and so there was a big counter. They used to take me in when I was about two, and I would stand on the counter and perform for the customers. My parents just took it as something that I did. I used to sing in Chapel. I was in the Chapel Choir and used to sing for birthdays, anniversaries and things. But my father never really thought that I could sing very well and... because I didn't sing the sort of jazzy things that he was into. He didn't really think I'd got that good a voice. It wasn't really until after the first album was released and suddenly from all over the place, people were getting in touch and saying, 'Wow! What a fabulous voice!' And I thought, 'Oh, maybe Dad didn't have it quite right after all.'

I was born and brought up in Cannock in Staffordshire. I just felt completely alienated there. I was a stranger in my home town. My father's grandmother was Welsh, although I never knew her because my father's father died when he was seven and he lost contact with a lot of that side of the family. It wasn't until after I moved to Wales that I found out that there were Welsh connections. But as a child I was always in love with Wales and I would cry when we had to come home from holidays. It was a place that I just felt such an affinity with. And then of course, one day I was at work, I was about twenty-one, twenty-two, and I was a teacher for the Coal Board, running their computer courses. And this bloke walked in on a computer course and I was completely and utterly dumbstruck. You know, Sicilian thunderbolt thing, where I thought, 'Well, I don't know who you are but I wish you'd do your shirt up a bit.' I was completely smitten.

The person was Rob and he was from Wales. After quite a long time, we did get together and I moved back to Aberdare in 1981. As soon as Rob and I met, even before we were together as a couple, we started performing together and doing covers at that point. That carried on when we moved to Wales. We married in 1982 and carried on singing and started writing together. I'd always, always, always written poetry from the moment I could hold a pen and I got to the finals of the Daily Mirror children's literary competition with the poetry and short stories that I wrote. So I started writing the lyrics and we wrote the music together. We performed in the Valleys, up and down Wales, in both English and in Welsh, because the first thing I did when I moved to Wales was to learn Welsh. I felt that I couldn't come and live in a country without making a big effort to be part of that country, so we moved here in the January and the next classes started up in the September.

I had the opportunity to go and do a degree. So I went down to Cyncoed and did an intensive two year B.Ed and taught in Lewis Girls' School in Ystrad Mynach, where I carried on with the singing, with the girls, because I started up a Welsh language drama group, although it was an English language school, and for three years we competed in the Eisteddfod. We came second in the second year we competed and in 1995 we won with a little musical sketch that I'd written for them.

Those girls that I taught way back in 1995 are still in touch with me. I still get Christmas cards from them all and we still meet up once a year and have a meal together and things. And most of them are still speaking Welsh, so I'm pretty proud of that.

Although we were performing all over the place, we'd never released anything. And it was coming up to Robert's fortieth birthday and he said, 'Do you know it's always been an ambition of mine to hear something that I'd written and recorded, played on a juke- box somewhere.' So I said, 'Okay then, let's go for it.' And he said, 'Are you serious?' I said, 'Yes! Go on then, go and find a recording studio, we'll do it.'

We recorded *Cleary's window'* and a couple of other tracks down at *Big Noise Studio*, which is now demolished, with Greg Haver who is now a close and very good friend. We released the single and things started to go a little bit crazy. We'd got play-listed on over forty radio stations in the UK, which doesn't happen when you haven't got a record label or any money or anything behind you. Unfortunately we couldn't do anything with it. We just didn't have the wherewithal to follow it through, but we were getting all sorts of nice press releases and things. We finished the album, it was a very, very low budget affair, largely due to Greg's generosity, because he really didn't charge us what he should have done.

We started gigging a little bit further afield, doing some stuff out of Wales for the first time. We did Middlewich Boat Festival which was surreal because we did one gig in the afternoon in the corner of a field on the hottest day for forty years... and we all melted in the corner there. Although we were gigging quite a lot we weren't really making any money at it. It's hard to make money from doing original stuff, particularly in Wales.

If you're singing in Welsh I think that there's an attitude that you should be doing it for nothing, for the love of the language. I do think that women musicians in Wales get taken less seriously than men, on that respect; they see it as a little hobby that you've got and you should be prepared to do it for the love of your hobby and for the love of the language... pat you on the head and they don't expect that they should pay you!

We recorded a second album and we just didn't have the money to release the thing. We'd got the recording and we were flat broke. So at that point I approached Dafydd Iwan at *Sain Records* and said, 'Look, here we are, here's what we've got. We don't even have the money to master the thing. Do you want to do it as a joint venture?' And he said, 'Yes, okay.' They took it on and did the mastering and paid for everything else that needed to be done and released it. I suppose that was 2001 and to our amazement, it went straight into the Welsh language charts at number eighteen. I happened to be making the Christmas cake at the time and when the charts were released on the radio, there I was... I was stuffing the chicken for Sunday dinner and making the Christmas cake at the same time, and the Christmas cake very nearly went in the chicken! I just couldn't believe that we'd done that well. Although we've not made hardly a cent out of it, it's gone round the world. In fact the stuff's probably being played more abroad than it is in Wales, which is crazy.

Last year was a bit bizarre because I got into the final six of the BBC's *End of Story* Competition and on the back of that I'm now several chapters into my first novel which is written in English, but set in the

Valleys. The Valleys are almost like a character in the novel itself, because it just influences me so much.

I decided that 2004 was going to be the year that I started to put myself first a little bit more. Because when you're a wife and mother, everybody else comes first and you're sort of bottom of the priority list. I just felt that there was an awful lot that I still wanted to do. And I'm approaching my late forties. I thought, 'Well, yes, you'd better get a move on girl.'

I'd rather be a person than an age, but still you are aware that you may not have as much time to do everything as you had when you were in your twenties. So I decided I was going to do some serious writing. To kick start that, there was a competition being run by the BBC to write the endings to stories written by eight famous authors. So I picked one by Marion Keith called *A Woman's Right to Shoes* and wrote the ending to that, more as a technical exercise to kick- start myself, than anything else. So I almost didn't post the thing off and having posted it off I promptly forgot about it. It was the end of July and we were gearing up to the National Eisteddfod in Newport where we were performing, and the week before we were due to perform I had a phone call from the BBC on the Saturday morning. Rob shouted me and said, 'Oh, there's someone from the BBC on the phone.' So I presumed it was to do with the Eisteddfod and didn't bat an eyelid. And it wasn't. It was this lady from BBC Scotland to tell me that I'd got to the final ten out of more than 17,000 entries. I talked to the woman on the phone, put the phone down and then burst into tears and just really couldn't believe it. So then they phoned me on the Monday and said, 'Actually you've made the final six, can we come and film you?'

They came down to the Eisteddfod and filmed the band performing and they filmed in the house, which was bizarre... I mean, what do you do if somebody's coming to film at your house? The house was cleaned to within an inch of it's life.

On the Tuesday I was told that I had to go down to London for the filming of the judging, where they were going to take six down to three. That was really horrendous, sitting in this pitch- dark room watching the video of the judges really tearing some people to pieces. I was very, very lucky. They were very, very kind to me, but some of the people there were really quite distraught at the comments the judges made. Then the following day we met Marion Keyes herself... who was lovely. Absolutely adorable person and very, very supportive. I didn't win, but I did make the final three and began writing my first novel which was sent to a literary agent, who replied to me within a week, giving me a list of things she wanted me to change. I've changed them and I'm currently in the position where I'm waiting for her to get back to me. It would be a bit like winning the lottery, because she said they get between two and three hundred submissions a week, and only took two authors on last year. We've decided if we can't get an agent interested, then we'll still publish the thing, either ourselves or through the Welsh Book Council. Having started the project I'll see it through. So that was that. Last year was a strange year.

Just as long as I can create. It's never been about money. It would be lovely to be able to make a living from what I do, musically and creatively. It's more difficult if you're a woman than if you're a bloke. I don't know why that should be, but you just don't get taken as seriously. So I do really take my hat off to all the women from Wales who have made it, because I know how hard it is. It's just part of the fibre of my being that I have to be creative. To not create would be like asking me to not breathe.

One of the most influential people, as regards attitudes, in recent years for me has been Rob's Auntie Brenda, who was an amazing lady. She was an actress and she performed in plays and things in the Valleys. Just before her sixtieth birthday she got her big break and she was on a television soap opera. Unfortunately, a few months into that, she was killed in a car accident. She was so full of life, very warm, very energetic person, who lived every second of her life. That taught me a big lesson because any of us could go at any minute and when you hold your slate up to say, 'What have I done?' I want my slate to be full. Not just with what I've achieved musically, or with the writing, but more than anything else with the friendships that I've made, because I really don't believe that you take anything other than the love that you have given and received during this life, with you into the next one.

If people remember me in fifty years time, I hope the thing that they will remember is, how much love I gave and received.

Songstress Update

Helen emailed to say that she has now finished her novel and it is currently with her agent. She is writing a welsh language version of the book over the summer. Her band *Dragonfall* are recording a new album in September, which will include a song that Helen has written about me, called *Sparkle Like Diamonds*. Thanks Helen!

PAT SMITH

PAT SMITH

Introduction

In my introduction, I discussed how Pat Smith was the first woman that I went to visit. I was hoping that although Pat was too young to be included in my original over 70 year old target group, she might be able to give me leads for my research journey. Pat was very helpful but as I listened to her experiences, it occurred to me that her history was equally as important to preserve. She inspired me to change my research remit.

As I met more and more women, I was amazed at the way their lives overlapped in time and how their insights, their shared experiences, fill out the picture of our history with more colour and texture.

When we arranged our meeting, Pat asked if we could include her musical partner, Mick Themes, as she felt he would be able to assist us. The pair have been in the band Calennig for 25 years, but recently Mick has been recovering from a stroke. We met at his sheltered accommodation, where he kindly allowed me to overview his personal library of traditional folk literature and to review his extensive lists of contacts.

Included here are excerpts from Pat's contribution during the meeting, regarding her life as a woman in music.

I went to the 16th Sidmouth (festival) with some old school friends. So, I would have been 18 years old, thinking I was going to a pop festival, and then when I came home, I found out my nearest folk club, but I didn't actually get into Welsh stuff until I met Mick. I've got to think now; you're going back a long time. Do you know, all I can think of are male performers. I can't think of any female performers. I mean there was one in my life, Maddy Prior, who I really worshipped at that time; in fact it's through her that I learnt to play the spoons.

I remember seeing *Steeleye Span* in Cardiff around about that time, and she played the spoons. A lot of people didn't know that she played the spoons, and that's the fist time I saw the spoons being played, and I thought I want do that and I did. I learnt the spoons, and then years later she came to my workshop at Bracknell Folk Festival .She came up to me at the end and she said, 'Oh, I've never seen spoons played like that before, where did you learn that then?' I didn't know her then, so I didn't like to say, ' I learnt from you!' It was a few years later that I got to know her, and I told her then, 'I learnt them from you.' But apart from that I can't think of any female singers really.

I wasn't working professionally when I met Mick; I was just going round the folk clubs doing floor spots, and just generally messing about really. We met at the Heath Ceileah. Mick was there doing a spot with Tommy Dempsey, and I was with Cardiff Ladies Morris Dancers. We got together then and started working together.

In fact, in all my experience of working with Mick, over 25years I often thought to myself, ' I'm the only woman in this concert,' or 'I'm the only woman in this particular festival.' There weren't women, were there? As far as I knew at the time, I was the only woman concertina player, for a long time. It was a man's world. It was mainly men.

I think, probably because the women were at home looking after the family, the kids, the house and the man went out; he had more free time I think to play music. Well, certainly from my experience, I had to juggle the music with looking after the house and my kids. I had two kids from when I was married. The only reason that I could work professionally as we did, was because my mother lived next- door- but- one and they used to stay with her when we were away doing gigs. I think that was the reason, because the women had to look after the kids, they couldn't go on the road and stuff. I was very lucky that I could do it.

Mick Themes: The men would be at work, in the mines, and the Welsh man ran things.

That's right, and in the evenings then, you'd all go down the pub and have a play and a sing, wouldn't you? But the woman was at home, looking after the kids. It was all male bars and women didn't go in then, they weren't desirable places.

I didn't think about it, I got on with men anyway, all my life I've gone around with blokes because I've had more fun with them.

When we went on tour, we used to go to Europe, used to go to Brittany and Holland and Italy and all these different countries on tour, but when we went to Europe when my kids were little, I used to take them with me and take a babysitter, that's how I managed. We did this mammoth tour of Belgium once, do you remember? We took Helen Flood with us as the babysitter. The babysitter's job was to look after my kids when I was on stage, and of course they had a free trip. That's how I managed, and then as they got older and they were in school, they would stay with my mother.

When we first started I was the only woman at the Sea Shanty Festivals. When we were doing the final concert on stage, sometimes it was all the men from the different shanty groups and me. I used to say I was the female cabin boy, but I used to get on with them all, you know. I'm sure that some of them secretly thought a woman shouldn't be involved in something like this, but on the whole they were generally fine. I mean, if they did think it they didn't say anything.

I was really, definitely encroaching on man's territory, but then as time went on, over the past 5-10 years, more women got involved in shanty festivals.

Mick and Pat kindly allow me to video them singing a song together. They sit opposite each other, face to face and Pat cues them in. Remarkably, despite his difficulty with the spoken word since his stroke, Mick sings fluently. It is a very moving moment for me as an onlooker: -

Soap, starch, candles, fender, brick and turpentine,
Pepper, glue and mustard,
And cod-liver oil and scent,
And black lead and clothesline,
Treacle, peas and fishing line,
Colours makes for painting, pots and brushes land.

Afterwards we discuss how it is that he can sing so well when his speech is in an earlier stage of recovery ...

See he can sing things like that and yet he has trouble speaking. When he was in hospital, I was working very closely with the therapists. She was nice wasn't she? I've forgotten her name, but I was working very closely with her and I used to go up the hospital and we used to spend an hour, me and her and Mick. I'd be teaching him under her instructions, and that brought him on that did.

Later, when we were leaving Mick's flat, I commented on how amazing it is that melody and lyric could have reached him in this way and how kind of her it was to spend that time with him to re-build his speech through song. She said that it was born out of her immense respect for him as a musician and his contribution to music that she would work with him, in the hope that he can restore the essence of what has been his life.

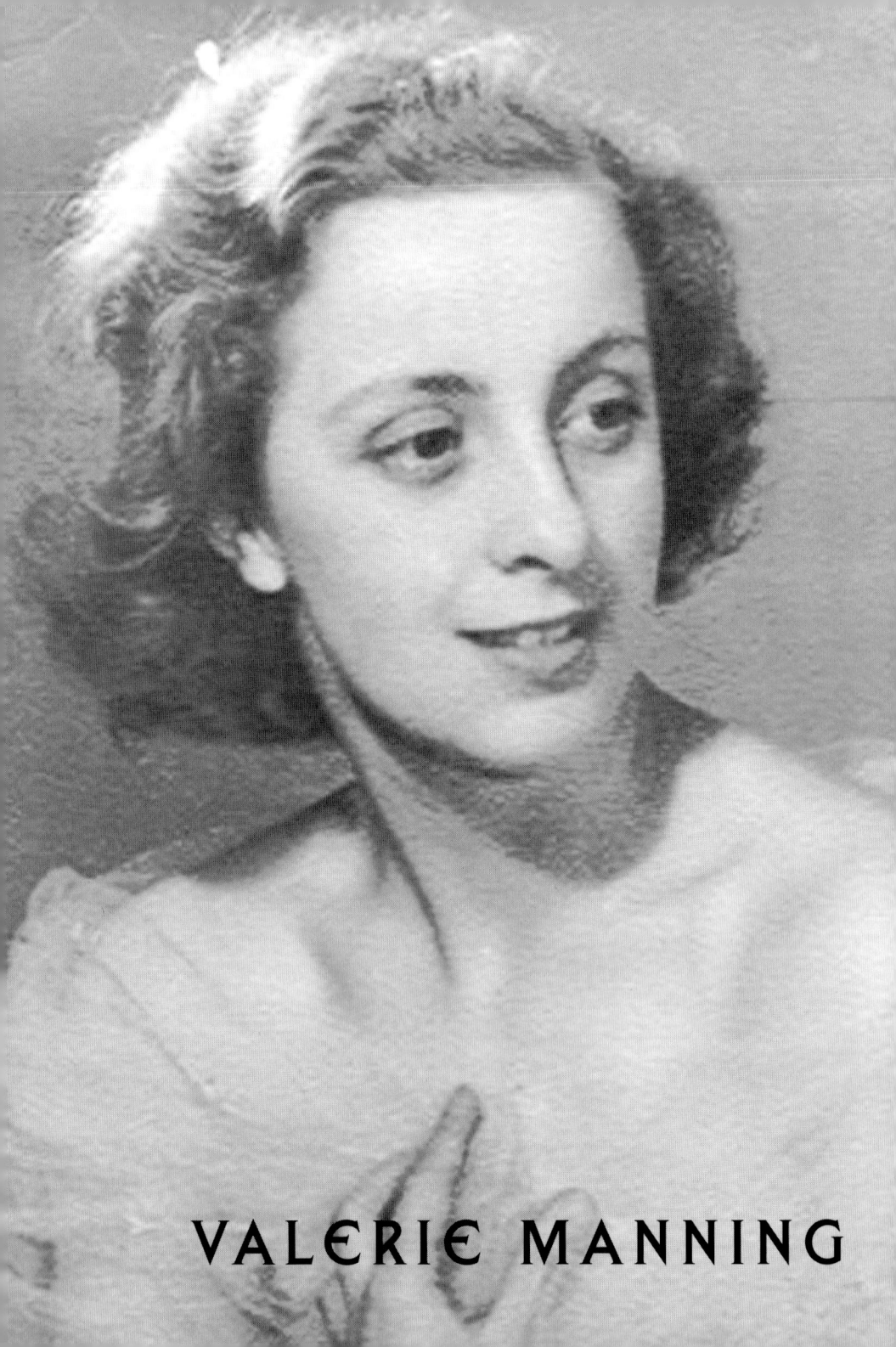

VALERIE MANNING

VALERIE MANNING

Introduction

Valerie's nature embraces, almost instantly. It was as if I had always known her. On the occasions that I visited her home, I was quite taken aback at how many people popped in to say, 'Hello.' Val is clearly a woman who cares deeply about others. Leading the Valerie Manning Singers has given her and her members, so much more than music.

I feel as though there was never a time when I didn't sing. I was quite shy as a little one. I was very much a daddy's girl, you see; I was the apple of his eye.

I can remember going to school and standing in front of the class and being asked to sing. This little top with long blonde curls. It went on through school. I would always be in the school concerts and it was taken for granted that Valerie would sing. And then I would sing in the local Eisteddfodau. The teachers would say, 'Oh there's an Eisteddfod; you really should sing there.'

In the war years, I was only a kid and my mother agreed with big trepidation, for me to sing in a dance band. I just about had a full time chaperone. I was twelve, thirteen perhaps?

During the wartime there were lots of dances going on. We had the town hall in Bridgend, and this was the place to have a dance. I sang with a dance band, which I loved. The chap who ran the band, he had a lovely wife, Phyllis. Phyllis always used to come with me in the car. She was always nearby like a chaperone. They would pick me up and bring me home. They made sure I was well looked after. My mother knew Phyllis so that was probably how I got away with that. I sat beside the piano when I didn't sing and when somebody said, 'Would you like to sing this number?' I knew exactly what to do and where to go. I was singing with the microphone and that was really grown up stuff. I loved that.

I was in the church choir of course, in Hope Church as a youngster. I had a dear friend, Iris, who didn't sing, but she was learning piano and I longed to learn. We didn't have one and I was fascinated with Iris playing. Then my mother bought a second hand piano, and before I started having lessons, I taught myself to play. I marked all the notes and what I didn't know, I asked Iris, because we were bosom pals. And remained so until she died a few years ago.

It was arranged that I would go to choir practice. Opera practice was going to be on a Monday night and choir was on a Tuesday. This was something without Iris, as Iris didn't want to come, and my mother wasn't entirely happy that I was going to go. However, Bill John came and saw her and said that he would take me, so he met me off the bus and took me to The York. I was fourteen. Well, when you think what they do at fourteen these days! So Bill took me over to the audition and I sang... they said, 'Oh yes, you're in.' So I was in.

I started going to rehearsals on a Monday night and we were going to perform The Arcadians in October at the cinema in Bridgend, which was a picture house but they had converted it during the war. We had worked our way through some of the music and the leading part, Sombra sang the *Pipes of Pan*. You've got to be on top of things to get through all those runs. The producers were Pat Mooney and his wife, Clovia. Mrs Evans played the piano wonderfully. A clever musician, she would go on forever. Leslie Evans was the Musical Director and he lived in Port Talbot.

So, it came to auditions and somebody said, ' Why don't you try for the part of Sombra. Apart from having sung in Eisteddfodau and the solos in school, I'd never performed in any sort of drama or acting, but I tried the audition. I went home, and at about half past nine that night, Mr and Mrs Mooney came to the house,

'We've come to say that Valerie has got the part of Sombre.'

My father was thrilled to bits. He was so proud, but he was a very quiet man, so he wouldn't say very much about it. I performed my part quite successfully, got some very nice write-ups and in the meantime, Clovia had again come to see my parents, to ask if she could have permission to give me singing lessons. I started having singing lessons with her, which was the early stages of my voice training. My voice had never been trained; I knew nothing about intonation; everything was natural at this point in time. There are vowels that you need to learn about and when you are only fourteen and have little experience, you don't know about these things. That was the start of my singing in light opera and then we went on to do an opera every year. Mr and Mrs Mooney also produced in Cardiff at *The Prince of Wales Theatre* and they were having problems finding a lead ...What did I do? ... They invited me up there to audition for that and I got that part. So that meant I was now going to Cardiff with the Cardiff Operatic Society and a member of Bridgend Operatic Society

I would have been seventeen, and I had a chance to pursue my career by going to The Guildhall School of Music. It was post- war and my mum just wasn't willing for me to go to London. It was much too far away and it was much too risky.

I was moving into the Cardiff scene. Someone said to me, 'You ought to sing with Welsh National, you should be singing with them.' So I went for an audition and I got in.

I started going to rehearsals with the Welsh National. I went to see the people who had auditioned me and they asked, 'Are you having your voice trained?'

I said, 'I go to someone that has been helping me with my singing.'

And they said, 'No, we mean professionally trained.'

I replied, ' She sang with the Carl Rosa Opera Company and she really has been helping me tremendously.' They suggested I went to The Castle, which was the new music college.

They said, 'I'll give you a note to introduce you to one of the tutors there. Get in touch with them and see if you can make an appointment to see him.' I thought, 'I've got to be able to afford this now.' We weren't a terribly wealthy family. My dad was working, but I didn't want to ask my parents. I was trying to be independent at seventeen and so I did it; I went along and I started doing some training on Saturday mornings. It was a bit difficult because in those days, I had to get the bus, and I had worked all the week, sometimes for a couple of hours on a Saturday morning as well. However, it all got a bit too much because I was singing with Bridgend Operatic Society, I was singing the Cardiff Operatic Society, fitting in those rehearsals, I was doing some solo work from time to time because people were now asking me to do things, and I was going to Cardiff to do those rehearsals. I was enjoying it thoroughly, but mixing with a whole new set of people and I was trying to fit in the lessons.

So something had to give. The Welsh National were an amateur group, at a professional level, doing full-scale operas and I had only just joined, so I decided to stop going, which I was very sad about. I think I went through a phase where I was disappointed that I hadn't gone to Music College.

I had already missed my opportunity to go to Guildhall because my mother hadn't been willing for me to go and this was my way of saying, ' Well, I'll do it my way!' Sadly, it didn't work out very well, so I think it was a difficult time for me.

I continued going to *The Castle* in Cardiff and doing the odd solo things and then I met my husband to be. Well, you know you start falling in love and things change a bit then. You loose your perspective. We were building this bungalow, where I still live; we were meeting new friends, going places and doing things, going to the theatre and there were other things on the horizon now. That was really the end of me performing, apart from the occasional solo bit here or there.

But I did get another chance to train. I was a mature student, it was 1964 and I'd had my second child, Mark. I was going to the college in Cardiff as a part-time student and enjoying it. I was then offered the opportunity of going to a conservatoire in Belgium at the suggestion of Sir Geraint Evans, who was listening to me singing whilst I was there with my tutor. My mother was quite keen for me to go this time. But I had two children; who was going to look after them? I would have to spend three months away from my children and this was an impossibility. My husband was in business and it wasn't a proposition. I had to turn it down. I went on doing things like singing at Brangwyn Hall, mostly operatic stuff, because that was my inclination … getting a good reception and encouragement to go on.

Then I started getting a hoarseness that was troubling me.

I still sang, which was wrong really and I eventually went to the doctors. After this persisted he referred me to a consultant and I had got nodes on my vocal chords. It was different surgery in those days. I was quite ill when I was having it done. I had my tonsils and these vocal chords removed at the same time. Then I had a haemorrhage and I was ill for quite some time. I suppose I never recovered and regained my singing voice. They said, 'Give it time and don't attempt to sing.' I rested my voice, but it didn't really return. I lost the volume. I can't sustain the sound any longer. It was quite a big voice despite the fact that I wasn't very big. I've got cuttings describing me as the golden voice soprano, but there you go, that was it…I survived I suppose, putting it at the back of my mind. I was a mum with two children; their lives were developing and my husband was in business and that was developing. The years passed by very quickly really. It was hard because since I was a little one, I had spent all my life singing.

One of the ladies who had a choir in town, whom I had known since I was a child, died rather suddenly and I went to her funeral because I had known her since I was a child. A couple of the ladies in the choir approached me and said, ' We have several concerts that we ought to be doing and would you consider taking us on as our conductress?' I had a long experience of music and singing in a choir but I hadn't conducted and I thought this might be the alternative for me.

I said, 'Well look, I will just do it for the twelve months to see you through.' It was a new experience and during that time several new ladies had joined the choir. The twelve months were up but I continued saying, 'I will see you through the Christmas concert, then I really am going to finish.. I had quite made up my mind. Then a couple of new ladies come over to me and said, 'Look, we so enjoy being with you and being with the choir. Won't you consider continuing?'

'No, I really won't consider.' I said.

'Will you come with us if we start a little group of our own, will you come and help us?' they said.

'Let's see the New Year in now and see how it goes. Let's suggest we meet again in February and I will see if I can have this hall and see if we can come back,' I told them.

So, they quickly spread the news around and a few of the ladies from that choir joined them. When I met them in February, we were eight, with no accompanist. They said that they would really like to do this, so I set about recruiting an accompanist, a friend I had known since I was a youngster, Olive. Her and her husband Jim had always encouraged my singing and we had done concerts together. I'd helped them with the Blind School Children's Choir amongst other things. So, I asked Olive, who was absolutely delighted, because by now Jim had died and sadly, she was on her own. The following week we met and I had managed to get some music. I was quite keen to teach unaccompanied singing which I loved, and that was it, it started with eight of us which grew to ten, which grew to twelve, and well, there you go.

The ladies decided they wanted to identify themselves as *The Manning Singers*.. I think it was in 1970. We grew and grew and then eventually we were fifty. We started concerts at local people's homes, and then we were invited to Germany on an exchange. We had a tremendous reception and had a really good time. All the girls enjoyed themselves and we stayed with German families. We had lots of fun, which we still recount. We began doing Annual Concerts, fundraising for local and National Charities.

A few years later the Air Born Division invited us to go to Holland. We went to the silent march at the cemetery and sang at the church where people had gathered when Holland was invaded. We sang at the hospital where our men were looked after when they were injured during the war. We left a brass plaque there saying, We'll keep a welcome in the hillside. We made them promise they would polish it. It was a wonderful experience. The ladies in the choir had worked hard and I had worked very hard to get them really on peak form. They did a wonderful performance, both in the church and the hospital. Again, lots of fun because some of us ended up in a Youth Hostel accommodation out in the woods, with only cold water. When we arrived, there were just bunk beds and if you were last in you got the top bunk. There were no sheets or blankets for us and I just wasn't having that for the ladies. Myself and the secretary were very cross with the chap behind the counter, who said he didn't speak any English. He did eventually agree and gave us some help.

We had a wonderful send off on the bus, all dressed up in our scarves. We had choir scarves made and we were all dressed up in various attire. It's just a hoot all the way, but when it comes to singing, they were absolutely spot on. We sang *God Shall Love The World* unaccompanied, and that really left a lasting impression on me as the sound of their voices was beautiful. They had worked so hard to achieve their pitch.

Our concerts continued and we had further successful tours of Brittany, France; and through this time we had annual dinners. We used to go out and enjoy ourselves. It's not just a choir; it's friendships that have resulted from this. We are just a very happy bunch of ladies and it is very noticeable. Everybody says, 'What a happy bunch of people you are, how lovely you all are.' That is very satisfying. I didn't take the career that I would have loved to have done but I really feel that maybe this was meant to be, this brings so much pleasure to so many people.

Valerie Manning Singers

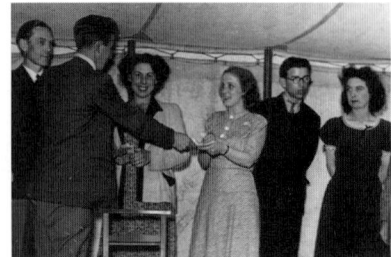

Valerie Manning

KATE STRUDWICK

KATE STRUDWICK

Introduction

Kate has a dedication to her work that clearly reveals her passion for arts in the community. Her innovative thinking within the field is nothing less than inspirational. Being in her forties before her confidence had blossomed as a performer, her experience is a lesson for others who wish they could muster up the courage or who worry that they are too old to join their first band. I agree with Kate, the music industry could do with a few more middle-aged women with attitude!

I was given a recorder when I was about 6 and although we did have occasional recorder lessons in school, most learning I did on the recorder was on my own. I used to play by ear, pop songs like *The Monkey's*.

I remember there was *The Six Wives of Henry VIII* on the television and that was really significant for me because that really got me into medieval renaissance music. I was really switched on by that. I joined the early music register. I wrote to David Monroe who did all the music for Henry VIII and I remember feeling absolutely distraught because he committed suicide. I couldn't understand how someone who was so talented, and so clever, and so admired in the musical world, would be so unhappy as to commit suicide. In those days, it was something I just couldn't understand, and I felt that the one person I'd really looked up to had gone.

While I was still in Exmouth, as a teenager, my brother, who'd taken up the guitar by then, mainly because he broke his leg and was bored, so he learnt to play the guitar while he was convalescing, and we found out that there was a pub that had a Folk Club on a Sunday night. It was well known for serving underage drinkers so we became regulars at the Folk Club. We used to go there, without fail, every Sunday evening, basically to have a drink but don't tell my parents that! And at the same time, we heard a lot of very good music. That's when I first started enjoying folk music. Being in Devon, there was the Sidmouth Folk Festival and my parents used to take us there to see the dancing. I was always interested in the music and the singing and also the rawness of some of the music reminded me of the medieval music.

I had started the flute when I was 12. I was living in North Devon at the time. In North Devon, it was a very small world. I was quite good at the flute for a girl in North Devon. I thought of going to University and I wanted to go back to Wales, where I was born. Cardiff was offering a musical course where you didn't have to be able to play the piano, and they also did a module on medieval music, so I thought that was the place for me. Actually, in many ways, it wasn't. I remember my first day at University the Professor saying to me, 'Now what grade did you get at A level?' And him saying, 'Well, that's not very good,' closely followed by, 'and what instrument do you play?' I said recorder and he just stared me out until I said flute. I knew I really hadn't got off on the right foot. Then the next question was, 'And I suppose you do play the piano, don't you?'

Well of course, I didn't and after that I was given piano lessons. The very sad fact is, that going to University put me off playing completely. I did my year of music and then switched to doing education and stopped playing altogether.

When I left university I went to work at Welsh National Opera. I remember actually saying to my boyfriend, who's now my husband, that there were only a couple of types of music that I could not enjoy at all and one of them was opera. Obviously, I had a crash course over 10years and I love it now. I was very privileged because I actually got to see a lot of rehearsals. I got to meet a lot of musicians. I got to meet a lot of very good singers and I suppose somewhere along the line that's what planted the seeds of what I do now. I had to come to terms with the fact that, although I'd been an average sort of flautist while I was in Devon, when I came to Cardiff, I really wasn't very good. Not good enough to become a professional flautist in an orchestra, which was the only sort of thing I'd thought of really. I wasn't going to perform but I was still very interested in performance and what makes people perform well. That was one of the reasons why I stayed so long in Welsh National Opera because I became fascinated by performers and all the things that can stop people performing well.

Most of my time at Welsh National Opera, I was an orchestra attendant, which is a roadie for the orchestra, so I was working for musicians all the time. Those are the days when Pavarotti kissed my hand.

I decided that I would like to get more into arts administration but found it very difficult to do that from being a technician. I realised I had to leave to get back into music and arts management. In those days, there weren't many courses you could do to get into arts administration, so I left and became a fundraising co-ordinator for the NSPCC, working with volunteer development. I did that for just over a year, and that gave me the opportunity to get the skills together that really influenced the big break of my career, which was getting a job at *Garden Festival Wales*. I managed to blag my way into a job organising the music. I was events officer for music and I think it was on the strength that I had worked with so many musicians, more than the fact that I had the contacts or the ability to do the job. I learnt on the job. That was a bit of a baptism of fire, but what a brilliant opportunity. I got to meet a lot of very good people, and I must admit, a person who was a great help during that time, was Geoff Cripps, who was also working at the Garden Festival. When I was at the Garden Festival I met Geoff, and Linda Simmonds and Chris Jones and I now perform in a band with them. They became great friends. I never played any music with them at all when I was at the Garden Festival. It was Chris who found out I played the flute and persuaded me to join him, doing some music to accompany a folk dance team, just as a laugh, after I'd finished at the Garden Festival. He'd nagged me for so long, that I thought, 'Oh! I'll do it just this once,' and that was, what? About 14 years ago.

It was a long, long time before I did consider myself as a performer. I think a lot of damage was done by that Professor. Quite honestly, in terms of confidence and all sorts of things. I think nothing gives me so much thrill as seeing my name down as a composer. It's something I never thought would be possible. The band plays all over the place, especially now we've got a website. We go to Ireland most years and play near County Ross Common and around that area. We've been to the Czech Republic and in September we're going to Germany for a few days as well. We get some quite interesting work and I really enjoy it.

Playing is very important to me now. I am passionate about it. I think the experience of working at the Garden Festival, and knowing what is expected of performers, working in difficult conditions, means that our band is probably quite employable. We know what people want and not just in terms of pleasing the public. It's not just what you play but actually being organised and turning up! There's always some poor sod organising it from that end, like we had to, and I suppose we understand it from their end.

It took me 20 years to get the experience to do this job as Arts Development Officer. You are working to increase access to the arts and participation in the arts. I really love it when people come in and share their enthusiasms and passions for the arts. We've had some fantastic projects here that have been a result of people sharing their ambitions. It's a bit like cooking. You have ingredients and sometimes, you can put two ingredients together that people haven't really thought might go together, and come out with something fantastic. A world without access to artists would be a very sad world indeed.

The role of Arts Development Officer is a relatively new concept. I know when the first ones came into Wales, because there was a bid to the Welsh Office jointly spearheaded by Valleys Local Authorities, and they got the money in December 1993. They were appointed in 1994 and that was the first Arts Development Officers in Wales. There's an Arts Management course now at the Welsh College of Music and Drama and I go there and give a lecture every year. I like to keep my hand in when it comes to organising large-scale live events, so I volunteer as the stage manager every year at the Pontardawe Festival.

Last year, I took quite a bold step in translating 13 Welsh folk songs that I thought people should have access to. I translated them into English as a stepping-stone for people to learn more Welsh, to make it a bit easier and get it away from the language issue. Just have a listen to this, it's a lovely tune; it's got good words, and it's quite fun to sing and when people are enjoying it, then gradually say, 'Have you tried this in Welsh?' I have written a couple of songs but they've yet to be performed by people. I haven't got the sort of voice myself to perform the songs that I write. I like to write for other people really.

I intend to grow old *dis*gracefully. I think I've been very, very lucky to be in the band I'm in. For a start it's unusual that, since Emma Trend has joined us, there are more women than men in it and we have a real equal part. Obviously, we're not there for decoration. Looking around at the bands, there are not many that have that sort of mix, especially in the Welsh folk scene. I think it's because testosterone always sells music. I think the type of music that women do, with Welsh music particularly, tends to be a bit girlie and doesn't have a lot of balls really. When I go to festivals it's nearly always blokes up there on the stage. There's not often middle-aged bints with attitude there; there's not many opportunities for them.

Our band is called *Allan yn y Fan*. We were a band with no name for quite a while and it used to just change every time we did a gig. Then, when I first had the offer to go to Ireland, we were rang up by this amazing person who said, 'Right, oh! I'm glad you'll do it, that's fine, what are you called? Because the poster goes to print tomorrow?'

So I just said *Allan yn y Fan* which means *we're going in a van.* It sort of stuck.

We've only just done our first recording last year. It's taken us that long to get our act together to do a recording. The CD's been pretty well received and we're thinking about doing another one next year. The CD is called *Off the map.* I must admit I had an absolute thrill when our CD was reviewed by Mojo Music Magazine and we got three stars. It was a positive review and I was thinking, 'My nephew's going to read this and think, Oh! it's Auntie Kate,' and I think that's great. Maybe it's deeply uncool to read Mojo now.

I don't have any children, so perhaps it's been easier for me, and I have a very supportive husband who lets me follow my creative urges. For the vast majority of women, that's not the case and for a lot of them, there wasn't any question of them going off and doing their career. They just had to put the career or their ambitions on one side, while they got on with the rest. But what I think is fantastic, is that they haven't abandoned those ambitions.

I think that people see us getting up there and giving it welly. Perhaps that's not what we are supposed to do. I was determined not to let the fact that I was a woman limit what I was doing. When I got the job as the orchestra attendant at Welsh National Opera, there was a sharp intake of breath from many a direction, because it wasn't considered a woman's job, heaving instruments around.

I think I particularly love being able to get on the stage and show off. It's not what women of our age are supposed to do and it's great.

Songstress Update

Congratulations! Kate has now successfully applied for promotion and is now the Arts Development Manager.

KATH ALLSOPP

KATH ALLSOPP

Introduction

Kath started her interview by saying that she didn't really know why Pat Smith had suggested her as someone for me to meet. She then told me her story and as it unravelled, it transpired that her life had almost always been interlaced with song. I find it quite telling that many of the women, with whom I recorded oral histories, felt that their contribution to song was not significant enough to be remembered.

When I was in school I was in an all girl band and we were only acoustic - 3 guitars, 6 girls - and we called ourselves *White Satin*. That was when I was about 15. I'm 49 now, so it was a few years ago. We started off going around church halls, old age pensioners, clubs, things like that; and then, as we got more used to being in public, we had a good range of voices and harmonies, so we started doing the British Legion, where we'd do the first bit before the main act. That was big time for us in those days. We used to have a change of clothes and everything. We'd go out in one set of dresses and go off. Then come back in with a second set and that's what we did. I don't think my mother was too happy but my dad was all for it, because he liked me singing a lot, and I couldn't do any wrong in his eyes.

I was always interested in playing the guitar, like I had a little tin guitar when I was 8, in London. Bought it in Petticoat Lane, busted by the time I got to Trafalgar Square. There were only 4 strings looped around 4 pegs and that was your set of strings. So there I was, hammering away on this thing. It came apart and dad fixed it.

Once I learnt how to play, of course there was this other girl who played and her sister played, and that was it. It went on from there, and we decided to have a go. They all disappeared. I had a card of them years and years ago, but I don't know where they are now. They're probably all in the 4 corners of the globe.

Then we had a manager, who was a friend of their's, and he used to make sure that we were alright, that we went to these bookings. He used to get me home, so I think my mum was alright about that. We got paid at some point, but not very much. It was something like 20 quid, which was a minor fortune for us in those days. We used it to buy things like an outfit. We'd say, 'Right ok, we'll put that money aside,' and go off and buy something.

Then I came up here to Cardiff to work in '71 and got into the folk scene a few years later. I just sort of gradually took on songs that appealed to me and then just worked my way into the groove I'm in now. I sometimes sing with a friend of mine called Stella, who is also a woman, and we get up and do a couple of harmony singings at the BBC club with Frank Hennessey on a Tuesday, once a month. I go to the Lyceum Tavern in Newport, we call it *Junction 26,* and in that club I would say we've got about 3 female singers and a dozen or so men. I don't know why, I think it's because women get scared of getting up there in public saying, 'Oh I'm not doing that.'

We've got some very nice harmony singers in the audience but they wouldn't get up. There's one girl who's sort of learning the guitar. Other than that she gets someone else to play for her, a man. There's another woman whose partner plays blues guitar. He accompanies her on occasions, or she sings unaccompanied and then there's myself and I do a bit of both, mostly guitar, but I have done unaccompanied when I'm pushed. I just never gave it a thought. I never thought it was a male domain.

I'd suss it out first, because I didn't want to appear pushy.

I wrote one song called *True Friends.* My husband died in '91 and I wrote the song 6 months later in that year, to thank my friends for what they had done and it just came out of that. It's been used several times, not recorded by other people but used to comfort other people, because they thought it was a very moving song. There was one woman who lost her husband - she was a pub landlady - and they asked if they could have a copy of the words to give to her. They framed it and put it up on the wall, which was rather nice.

I think when my husband was alive he'd come to gigs with me. I would have a lot of nerves beforehand, and I'd be very often in the car doubled up, and be in agony with stomach cramps, which was only nerves, because once I'd have started setting up, or started singing, it would sort of go. And then, after he'd gone, I went through a phase. I was in the pub in my local, didn't sing for months, didn't pick up a guitar, didn't do anything, and then my friends cajoled me into doing it and said,

'Go on get up there.'

One of the big songs I had was *Working man.* It became my song; everybody associated it with me. So then I got persuaded to play it in this pub one night. I did one line and I couldn't remember. I had to stop and start again but once I did that, I was ok. The strange thing is, that when I was going through setting up equipment, my nerves weren't there. I didn't feel anything and I just thought, 'Why am I doing this?' It was really weird but it was almost like, because he was there, he'd be more critical of me, and I think that after, I relaxed a bit more, after knowing that Ken wasn't there, but at the same time he was very proud of what I did you know, and other people said I've improved since then. It's weird.

'It's almost like you just take it on board now, and your presence on stage now is better,' they said, 'you come out on stage now and you're in command.' How true that is I don't know.

I was in the festival at Pontardawe, in the club tent, and it was my turn to get up and do something. People just drift in and out when they want, and they drifted in and just stayed in, which was nice, and then I got them singing part of the song .It was a *la di da di da* bit for them and I said, 'Do that bit again,' and they did it. I thought ooo! It was just for that 3 - 4 minutes. I had total and utter control of the tent. You know that something has gone really well and the hairs stand up on the back of your neck and you think, 'Oh god, this is amazing,' and when you get a buzz like that, I suppose you just think, 'This is why I do it, not for money.' I wouldn't say that I'm one of those people who's got to get up on stage, but I really love it when I've done it.

I'm quite willing to do it for a ticket. If they say, 'Come along for a half hour spot and we'll give you a free ticket,' then fine. If I get paid it's a bonus.

I think it was very difficult for women to break into any music scene, not because they had to be better, but because they weren't really accepted. It's only the last 10-15years that women have started slagging off men in a song, saying, 'We can do this,' or 'We can do that and the men can't.' It wouldn't be done before. You wouldn't do that. A lone man could get up there and just do it, but if a woman did, it would be more difficult, because they are expected to sing a different type of song.

If she didn't appeal to the men, then she wouldn't get on at all. I think it's the same in clubs. If you see women singing, it takes a very clever woman to be able to appeal to the men on a sexual basis, you know good looking, singing raunchy songs, but also to get the women on their side and turn things round to say, 'We have a lot to put up with,' so they get both on their side.

A good voice, I don't think, is enough always and I think over the years, I've tended to put in some more humorous material, because that appeals, and that sometimes goes down, not better, but you get their attention. You can sing a very good ballad, then all of a sudden, you put in this little funny song, and you've got them. I think that helps, so I do a bit of comedy.

Like you say about an emotional journey, a song is where you take someone to another place for 3 minutes and then bring them back again. When you sing songs, sometimes they are so emotional, that you can't sing them without going there yourself, and the only way to deal with that is to, literally, cut the wires, so that you're singing it outside of yourself. There may be one particular verse where you think, 'Oh God, every time I hit this I'm not going to do it.' So basically you've got to detach yourself, not easy sometimes. I think you sort of improve over the years. I hope. I think my voice has got slightly richer than it used to be, probably because of age as well, you tend to get a little bit lower than you were, but at the same time, I think your presence and everything else improves as well. Other people have noticed I'm coming out with an air of so-called confidence. They can't see my knees shaking.

It was a gradual thing. It takes a long time for some self- belief. Like you know you've got a good voice, or you know that you've got a reasonable voice, but very often it just comes around when people say, 'That was ace,' you think, 'Thank you.' It takes you back a little bit sometimes.

I've done 2 CD's. One with a friend of mine, Julie Forsyth, who is now in Scotland. She moved away a couple of years ago. We started singing together because she came to the Lyceum folk club and didn't have a guitar accompaniment. Somebody suggested that I knew some of the stuff she did, so we had a quick practise in the corridor, ran through a number, and then we'd do a few things together. That worked out quite well and in the end we decided we make a CD called *Love n all that*, we discovered that all the songs were about love, and all that. The song that I wrote *True Friends* is on the CD.A little while later, about a year, although I'd met this woman before, Anne, we sung together in Miskin Folk Festival. She sang and I harmonised, usually rehearsing down the phone. She might say, 'Do you know this song?' and she'll start singing it and I say, 'Oh yeah, I think I've got that,' and she says, 'Well look it up and we'll get together and sort something out.'

Then we made a CD together and we became known as *Kathannie*, which is hardly an original name, but we didn't know what to call ourselves at the time. The emblem on the front of the CD is a model of the *Harry Prigg Memorial Trophy*, which was originated in The Miskin Arms by one of their regulars. In memory of him, they decided to award this for the best song of the weekend at the Miskin Folk festival, and on that CD, is a song called *Loving Hannah*, which is a traditional song. Annie and myself sang it together, unaccompanied, and we won the Award. That was the first time it was initiated. I think it was 1996/7. It's been awarded every year since.

For Annie and myself, that is our song.

I always thought that if I got the boot from this place, and they said, 'Alright, that's it, we don't need you anymore,' I would go to Ireland and have a go. Why Ireland? I don't know, but I think that there is a lot more interest. They're much more prepared to have someone sat on a stool and carry on. Irish people like to sing.

I think it would be difficult to live without song. Somewhere along the line, there's got to be music in my life, somewhere. If I watch television at 12 O' Clock at night, by 20 past I'd be asleep, but if I was playing music or playing my guitar, it's more likely to be 4 in the morning, because it just goes on. You think, 'Oh, I'll just play one more song then I'll go to bed.'

Album Cover

BUDDUG LLOYD ROBERTS

BUDDUG LLOYD ROBERTS

Introduction

The second songstress introduced to me by Roy Sear, was Buddug Lloyd Roberts. Buddug has been secretary of the Welsh Folk Song Society for over 30 years. The Society is celebrating it's 100th Birthday.

Sitting by the piano in her front room, Buddug reminded me of the rose that stands in the corner of the garden. An unassuming rose, that has always been there and has an inherent beauty. Not a beauty that shouts loudly from the flowerbeds or that just comes and goes with a flash of colour and then disappears, but a dignified rose, with roots that reach out across the garden, holding everything together; one of the mainstays of the garden that you can rely on to add grace. Our Welsh Rose.

My upbringing was in a very Welsh community, in the slate quarry district in Ffestiniog. We sang in school, and I learnt to play the piano. I suppose I would be about 10 years of age. Later, I took what is similar to the O-levels today, what we called the Centre Welsh Board. I had a credit in music, then I went to the training college and did music there.

The National Eisteddfod came to Pwllheli, that was 1955, and I was friendly with a teacher from the next village. He was teaching music in Porthmadog. I used to go there. He had a ladies choir, singing mostly Cerdd Dant, you know, the Penillion. When the Eisteddfod came to Pwllheli he said, 'Why don't you compete?'

Well, I couldn't compete in the solo, the really classical competitions, and he said, 'Why don't you compete in the folksong?' So I said, 'Well, why not, I'll have a go.'

I learnt two folksongs, went off to the Preliminary Test, and lo and behold, I found myself on the stage. Well, talk about stage fright! Of course, I was on the stage on a Thursday afternoon, just before The Chairing Ceremony, and The Pavilion was absolutely crammed with people. There were three of us on the stage, and when I was called forward, I had no idea what I was supposed to sing. I'd just gone absolutely blank. Oh! it was a terrible feeling. Anyway, fortunately Huw Jones, who was conducting the competitions that afternoon, he said, 'Just a minute, sit down there because I want to announce something or other,' So, I sat down and thought, 'I must take hold of myself and do something.' I felt so stupid. Anyway, I managed to get through it and I came 2nd. Emrys Jones, who'd been doing a lot of Cerdd Dant and folksongs, singing for years, he beat me by a mark. After that I started competing, not straight away, because I got married and had a child.

I competed in two or three Eisteddfodau. I believe in South Wales, I came 2nd about three times, and then in 1965 I said, 'Right, this is it; I'm not competing anymore after this year,' and I competed in Newtown. I got the first prize there. All the family said, ' Now we'll have some peace and quiet! '

Of course, following that, I did quite a few radio spots. I used to go down to Cardiff for the television programmes. Back then, they were all live. They weren't recorded, so if you made a mistake you'd had it. I must have been singing on the radio and somebody in Bangor said, 'You should make a record.' So I did one for children, aged 4 up to 7 years old, which has been quite popular, called *Helo Blant*. Eleanor Bennett accompanied me on the harp. I went into a hall in Porthmadog and we recorded the nursery songs straight away, not in lots of takes, no fuss, because the acoustics of the hall were all right, apparently.

It was well accepted and it's still being sold in the music shops today. There are so many people who've said to me, 'We get you for breakfast, dinner, tea and every time we go in the car, we get you.' I don't know if that was a compliment or not.

After that they asked me to do an adult album. It was released by a recording company called *Cambrian*, which were based in South Wales. They went out of business and so *Sain Records* took the children's one.

I was a teacher and a Centre in Gwynedd asked me would I prepare a book of Folksongs? I prepared a book and that seemed to be well received, so they asked me to do another one. I did four in all and then after that, a friend of mine in Anglesey prepared a simple piano accompaniment to go with the four songbooks. These were used by teachers in schools. Unfortunately that centre closed down because of lack of money, like a lot of places.

I had a ladies choir for a while and we would hold concerts singing Cerdd Dant as well as Folksongs. I don't know of course, but some of the songs being very emotional seem to appeal more to the women. Many of the men who sing folksongs tend to enjoy singing the lighter side, the ballads, but as I say, the ladies seem to go in for the more emotional or sad songs, and are more able to express those feelings.

I used to go to sing in St.David's concerts, and by then I was on the committee of the Welsh Folksong Society. I've been a member now for 40 years or more. It's become a part of my life really. It's enriched my life definitely. I became the secretary and have been for nearly 30 years, I should imagine. Emrys Cleaver, who used to live in Cardiff, was the secretary for years. He was getting on, so he pushed the job on me. I've been in touch with so many people. I used to get letters from the States, from Europe, inquiring about different folk songs, very interesting.

I've had a lot of pleasure and I've been reading so much about the early position of the Folk song. At the beginning of last century there was a Methodist revival, people just didn't sing folk songs. They thought they were very, very bad. I've been going around telling people about our history because I think it's important to understand the position of folk song at that time, especially with young people. I've talked to the students in Bangor over the years, to the teachers there, because there was no traditional music in the music department. Now, you've got Wynn Thomas and Stephen Rees, and they do a lot; it's part of the curriculum. It's surprising how many young students have finished the course and would come on the phone with me and say, 'Can you give me some information about.....' That's my interest. I've also been a member of the Eisteddfod Council, for some years now, and the panel that's attached to the Council when we go through the programmes for the Eisteddfod every year, and I've been a chairman of the committees.

I don't sing as much now but I'm still involved in song. I've been playing the organ for about 50 years. Every Sunday people say, 'Don't you feel you'd like to give up?' I say, 'No, I'll continue for as long as I can.'

Songstress Update

When I caught up with Buddug, she was very busy with music projects in her local community, trying new creative avenues to keep Welsh folk song alive.

Buddug in the Choir

GERRI SMITH

GERRI SMITH

Introduction

My friend, Mary Jefferson, told me about Gerri. When we met, her elegance and beauty intertwined with an unexpected quirkiness. Funny and good fun, Gerri is a songstress who has cleverly created her career in song by thinking outside the box.

I was brought up in a little Welsh village just outside Pontaddulais, Hendy. When I was about 3 or 4, my mum used to insist that I could do anything. I was quite a performer when I was a very tiny little girl. I don't know who I take after because both my parents were brought up in orphanages. I suspect a musical influence somewhere in my family history that we don't know about. It would be fascinating to try and find out. It's possible these days. My mum certainly never sang. I never heard either of my parents actually singing. My brother has got a beautiful voice, so it must have come from somewhere.

Fantastically, with coming from having nothing, a lot of my relatives have done very well. Both my parents said they had a good basic education in an orphanage and one of the other influences of course, was that my mum used to be a maid in a household that had lots and lots of money. She believed she knew exactly how to behave, how to lay the table, how to dress.

During the war, Swansea was bombed very badly and our house was full of my relatives constantly being evacuated to our two bedroomed, two up, two down, house. I had an upbringing that was a very extended family.

I was the first of my family to go to a Grammar School, the very first. There were lots of children who looked up to me, because I was the first to go to Grammar School. I didn't know that at the time. It was years and years later, when we were having a chat one day, and my cousin said, 'Oh well, you were always being thrown at us as an example! If Gerri can do it, you can.'

In those days we were all churchgoers. I went to a local church three times on a Sunday. Most of what you did in the village was connected with the church. I was a member of the drama society, so I was on stage at 10 for the first time. I used to sing constantly. I went to Llanelli Girls Grammar School. It was a wonderful all girls school, and we had a very strong drama section. There were performances every year by the school in one thing or another, and the first time I can remember singing in the school I chose, I think; *that I Shall Never See a Poem Lovelier Than a Tree.* I can remember singing that song very clearly up on the stage. I remember that I didn't go to school on the day that my team were presented with the award for the Best Direction and the Best Actress was me. I wasn't there to get my prize, which taught me never, ever to skip going anywhere again.

The headmistress of the school who was a lady called Thea Jones, who was a very famous headmistress actually, she sat me down and asked me what I wanted to do and I wanted very badly to go on to a theatrical school. In those days we weren't encouraged, it was, ' Oh dear! Can your parents afford to send you to drama school?' And I knew my parents couldn't. Obviously, I wasn't as keen as I thought, because she put me off by saying that I would never earn anything! So I didn't go to drama school. I went into the Civil Service, got married, and brought up my children.

I had four children, and it wasn't until I came back to Wales that I thought, ' I want to go back into the theatre.' So I joined a local drama company and did lots and lots of things constantly. My kids were now 5, 9, 11 and 13, but I still managed to go out, with a very supportive husband, and I did quite a few musicals in that amateur company. I decided that I wanted to do something on my own as well. So I wrote a one-woman show, called *A Bird's Eye View.* All the songs were written by women and it was about women: a look at women through women's eyes. I did a lot of Mae West particularly, because I thought Mae West was an incredible woman. I sang saucy, racey songs, and I took it round mainly to women's groups. I wasn't paid very much for it. They paid my expenses and things like that.

I was working then, on a semi-professional basis in Cardiff, at the Sherman Theatre, and I was doing a lot of work with a post-grad company that Geoffrey Axworthy had set up. I worked with a director and he said, 'You know, you should really get your equity card Gerri.'

In those days you didn't get an equity card unless you worked for 16 consecutive contracts, no matter what. It was very difficult and each theatre was given an allocation in a season. It was Gareth Armstrong, who was the Welsh director that said, 'Ok, I'll give you an equity card.' That's when I became a professional actress.

It was 1987, so my kids were grown up. I was in my 40s and I set out on a new career. I was still doing this one-woman show as well, more often now. My very first real good part was in a chorus at Theatr Clwyd.

We did a number one tour with it. That was a four-month job. I was away from home, and the kids. I had a wonderful time, I loved it, great people in the play, very good director, lovely people, and I'm a still friend with some of the people who were in the play.

In all aspects of this business called acting, you do have an awful lot of time when you're not working, unless you are extremely lucky. You have to really do a lot of thinking about how you're going to get on stage and what you're going to do and how you can perform if you're not being employed. I saw an advert in *The Stage* for a murder mystery company, and they wanted a lady who could sing. I went along and did an audition and got the part of the leading lady in a murder mystery cabaret. We did 10 murder mysteries a year if we were lucky, but I remember the lady telling me she was going to make me a star. It was corporate entertainment. She ran a big corporate entertainment company. She'd bought a plot, which involved Lady Julia and her company coming to the hotel to perform a little concert in memory of her deceased husband and then the murder evolves during the meal. The band performed a little concert, so I had to sing a couple of songs. I enjoyed doing that very much.

As a member of equity I used to go to the equity meetings and I became secretary of the equity branch in Cardiff. I met another actor, who was doing corporate stuff, and I told him about these murder mysteries I was involved in. And this is fate, because I believe in fate. He rang me up the following week and said, 'Oh Hi Gerry, I remember speaking to you last week and you told me you were doing murder mysteries and I've just been asked to do one for a company. I don't know anything about them. Could we get together and maybe put one on?'

I said, 'Oh! Yes, I'm sure we could.' We couldn't use their plot, so we had to find another one. I rang up a friend in Bristol who was a writer and said, 'Look, I want you to write a murder mystery for me that contains a cabaret act. I know how it should work because the one I'm doing doesn't work very well."

So he wrote us a plot, very simple little murder mystery with a cabaret. It was hugely successful. We performed it to Thorn EMI and they had about 140 people there. They thought we were wonderful. We went to a local hotel and said that we'd got an evening's entertainment, and if they put it on, we'd do it for nothing for the first time. It went like a bomb, and we've been at this hotel for 15 years now. We still perform there, because the hotel rebooked us and paid us and that's how *Murder on the Menu* grew. They book us 4 or 5 times a year and we have to have a different plot every time we go there. It's like a play season but the wonderful thing is, that I sing all the time. I love acting and I love singing, so it is combining those two things. We have an absolute ball doing them because they're great fun. I never actually tried writing the songs but I know so many.

Whilst singing, people would say to me, 'Do you know you look like Vera Lynne?' I couldn't see it myself, and then fate again. In 1991 there was an advert in a Cardiff newspaper saying that a new programme called *Stars in their Eyes* was coming to Cardiff to audition. I went along for the audition and they were totally and absolutely gob-smacked. They said, 'We don't have to do anything to you. You look like her you sound like her.' I got on straight away, so in 1992 I went on *Stars in Their Eyes* as Vera Lynne.

I then joined a couple of agencies as the look-a-like Vera Lynne. Especially in 1995, I sang all over the country for all the V-day celebrations. Everywhere I went I had wonderful experiences, because the old people think of Vera Lynne as still being in her 40's, as she was. They've got this vision of her, so they really believed I was her, although she's 80 years of age now. They would come up and say to me, 'Oh dear Vera, if it weren't for you we wouldn't have won the war.'

There was a wonderful story when I was in Salisbury doing a Vera Lynne big concert for VE day, and it was the day after she'd appeared in the Imperial War Museum. She was 70 odd, and this gentleman came rushing up to me and said, 'Oh Dame Vera, could you come and have a word with my mum, she was in Burma, same as you.' So I had to go up and speak to this lady. This happens to me lots and lots of times. You can not go up to old people, who think that you are the person and say, 'Don't be silly.' You just have to pretend, and she took my hand, I was nearly in tears because she said, 'My husband and I were in Burma, and he died soon after, and I saw you on telly last night in the Imperial War Museum and I've just sent my memoirs and nobody knows what you and I have been through, because you were the only star that came out to Burma.'

In 1997 I read in the Western Mail that Dorothy Squires, who was my mum's very favourite star, was living with a fan in the Rhondda Valley. I decided to commission somebody to write her life story. I took the show up to Edinburgh. I'm still doing Dorothy and I've just done a drama series, which is going to come out in June. I set up a web site. The BBC found it and said, 'Oh my god, we're looking for a Dorothy Squires look-a-like for a series that's coming in June called *The Long Film*.'

In years gone by, I think it was a lot easier for men to go onto stage, as it always is. There are more parts for men, no matter what age you are, but if you think and look back, women with determination do what they want, need to do. I've always felt independent. I think that there are obviously lots and lots of people in my era who thought they couldn't do things. Money was more of a barrier for me. I mean if my parents had been wealthy, I've no doubt that my headmistress would've said, 'Oh, you can afford to go.'

There was the attitude that if you chose to be a wife, it is a full time job, but I never felt I couldn't go off and do things. If I had been married to somebody who was not supportive, I'm not sure what I would have done. You do have to have a partner who is supportive and these days most men seem to be very supportive of women. Certainly my children are married and the girls are incredibly more successful than my boys. My boys are very supportive of my daughter-in-laws and do as much in the house. Although my husband was supportive, he never changed a nappy. Lots of people used to say, ' Oh you're lucky, Joe lets you do anything,' and I used to say, 'I beg your pardon! He doesn't let me do anything. I do what I want to do. How can he let me do.' It is an attitude. If you're the sort of person who believes you have to have permission to do things, then maybe you won't do it.

I don't think that it's a myth that the Welsh are a musical nation. I was surrounded by music. Not by my parents. There was a male voice choir in the village and I used to adore it, absolutely love it. As a teenager, my brother was a member of the choir, and I used to go and listen to them. After rehearsal they used to come to the pub and I would sit and listen to them. Wherever you go, the Welsh will manage to dominate the harmonies, so it's definitely a part of what I am really, isn't it? I have a strong feeling of being Welsh. Although, I really do believe that over the last 20 years, Welsh language has divided us rather than united us, because there are more people in Wales who cannot speak Welsh, but who are Welsh, than there are Welsh speakers. I believe Welsh should be taught in schools and I think it's a part of our heritage, but to me I think, please God, let us have all one language. In this small island of ours, our Welsh accents and our Scottish accents and all our various regional accents, make us pretty unique anyway. We can establish where we come from. You can always hear the Welsh lilt you know. My father came to Wales when he was 12 and died here at 83.You could still hear his cockney accent. Whereas, my mum was born in Wales, but from Lancashire parents. We're all a huge mixture, so I suppose there's all sorts of influences in every part of us.

Singing is a source of joy to me, although my taste in listening to music can be quite wide. I am a pop singer of my generation. Pop music today leaves me cold mostly, but just like the kids of today, who know all the words to all the songs in the hit parades, I know all the words to Frank Sinatra, Rosemary Clooney, Ella Fitzgerald, all the wonderful singers of my era. I know that music and I adore it. I love to dance to it. It's a fantastic thing to have the reaction of an audience. You walk off the stage and you have no idea what the reaction will be. With a nice round of applause, sometimes it is fantastic. Without music in my life, it would have been very much less bright. It evokes romance. It evokes sadness. You can listen to an upbeat thing and suddenly feel great. It gives you great energy.

Without music in your life, it would be awful wouldn't it? But I can remember thinking, ' My God, if I didn't have children, how terrible it would be,' because being a mother is a truly wonderful thing. You have to make the most of everything that you have in your life.

Gerri Smith

BERYL PAINTING

BERYL PAINTING

Introduction

Amanda Painting contacted me by email, telling me about her mother, Beryl. When we spoke, Beryl felt that although she'd really like to be included, her interview may not be relevant because she was not Welsh nor Welsh speaking. I asked her how long she had lived and performed in Wales and she replied, 'Only 45 years.' I find it very interesting that some of the women I interviewed, despite having performed and/or written in and about Wales, for or all their lives', or at least for a large part of it, felt that they may not be 'Welsh enough' to be included in a book about Welsh women's history of song. Reasons they gave were: that they were not born Welsh speakers, or not born Welsh, or had learnt Welsh as a second language or were no longer living in Wales. Just maybe, one of the reasons that our history is, as The Western Mail observed when reviewing my research, 'strangely silent' has to do with a dilemma women face, regarding whether or not their contributions are eligible to be recorded and if so, where they should be placed.

Well, if I begin at the beginning - nearly all my family are musical. My mother missed it, but her father, my Grandfather, was the tenor in the local choir and he used to win the cup at the *Singing Festivals* in England. My mother couldn't sing a note and she was always so disappointed that she couldn't sing. So she always encouraged me. I had singing lessons from being a little girl and joined choirs and things like that. Music has been right through my life, really. I love singing and I like listening to all the bits and pieces, but it is the history of folk that I would say has had the greatest impact.

We sang all the traditional English folk songs in the school choir. I'm 72 now ... so it's going back sixty years. I had a lovely teacher, when I was in school. She inspired me. She was a brilliant pianist, Miss Birtwhistle. And you know we'd talk, and she'd always say, 'Oh, you've got a lovely voice, Beryl.'

When the war ended she came in dramatically and she said, 'Now girls, we must sing.' It must have been VE Day. The news had travelled very quickly and got to school.

Miss Birtwhistle said, 'Now we've got to sing and put our hearts into it.' And you could see that she was all emotional and playing the piano and conducting. That was one of the things that I'll always remember, a very vivid memory of Miss Birtwhistle, who was absolutely wonderful.

I would say, during the war there wouldn't be much of singing lessons going on. But there were lots of choirs and actually if you got a good conductress, she'd be a trained vocalist at some point and she would get you to breathe where you should and to open vowels where you should, and do all of these things. So, basically, if you were in a good choir with a good conductress, it was as good as having singing lessons.

I play that guitar over there. I haven't done it for ages, although a lot of the folk songs that I sing are better on guitar and don't sound so good with a piano. But what I found with folk, I like the old ones, the ballads, and the love stories because they tell a story. They have a beginning and an end. And as regards the shipping and sailing, a lot of the cabin boys would go out to sea – girls dressed as boys – and you know it's a twist in the tale. Like *The Chastity Belt Song*, that's a very funny one. And they actually sound better on a one-to-one playing a guitar, and a small audience.

When the children were very young I learned a few nursery rhymes, like *Bobby Shafto* and *Hickory Dickory Dock* – all those with three chords and you could just play those and they'd join in. And then I got a little bit ambitious and did four chords and then I wanted to know how to do a bit of 'plucking' and yes, so that was how I started with a guitar. And we used to have a lot of visitors in the evening, and we used to have sing-songs.

And then I joined the local concert party, the Theatre Mawldan, and we used to go round to the old folks and entertain. They got an opera group, *Opera Teifi*, and so I sang in that.

I sang in about three different choirs and usually got the solo bit, singing soprano. And then I decided to go and have some lessons, which I did with a tutor from Aberystwyth University. He lived in Aberaeron and I used to go to him once a week. The cost of the lesson, this is going back a bit, was £5, so my husband used to love to tell people that I went to a tenor for a fiver.

More or less the first lesson he said to me, 'Now Beryl, your mistakes are with you and the only way we can erase them from a singing point of view, is that you mustn't sing any of your old songs. But I want to give you something entirely new, something you've never heard of – we're going to put the new method of singing on to it until we've got it perfected … and then you can go back to your old singing.'

So, I had to learn the pronunciation and the breathing and all the rest of it. And I did that for a long time. I used to love to go for my lesson. I really loved it. And then I found out when I went back to the guitar and I started doing folk, it just didn't ring true any more, because I couldn't stop doing the classical. I just stopped playing the guitar as much as I would do normally, plus the fact I was doing so much singing, I hardly had time for the guitar and playing.

And then about seven years ago, I had arthritis and that just put a stop on everything. The choir said, 'Oh Beryl, we'll put a chair there for you. It doesn't make any difference.' And I said, 'No, I wouldn't like that, sitting on a chair in front of the choir singing.' So I let that go. But I did a lot of Old Time Music Hall.

I did a week of jazz at the Isle of Wight and a week of Noel Coward through the Women's Institute, at Abingdon, which is their WI College, and they give a bursary each year. Literally, it's just your name coming out of a hat; you don't have to do anything to win it. But I won the bursary that particular year and they were doing a week of Noel Coward - all the experts are there.

I've mixed around and done all sorts of music and really enjoyed all the things that I've done. But I think I'm what they call a nervous solo singer. I can sing and play here, without any problems, but if you took me to a little theatre or put me on a stage, suddenly, I can't remember the next line. And if I was singing two songs, I can't remember. And I think, 'Ohhhhh!' So I'm not good at entertaining a wider audience, but I'm okay with a duet or a quartet, or anything like that - I'm fine.

We use to hold regular weekly soirées, here, at the guest house. I'd have six or eight guests, and usually we have some campers from our field. We'd say, 'We'll have music later on tonight.' We used to do a lot of sea shanties.

I never thought to be a professional singer. One of the first things my last singing teacher said to me was, 'Well, I can't understand why you've never wanted to be a singer. You've got a lovely voice.' Then he said, 'I can't understand why you've let that go and you don't want to do it.'

And I've always said the same thing, 'No I don't. No way. I'm too nervous and I'll never get over it. I really won't.'

The first time I was left on my own to sing solo, I just stood on stage as stiff as a little soldier and sang. And if I could have run off, I would have done. You know, it was awful.

When I was in my fifties I made friends with a fantastic pianist and she used to go dancing to Aberporth to a dancing club. And she came home very excited when I was going over for rehearsals. She said, 'We've got a new couple who've joined the club and he does a lot of

Gilbert & Sullivan.   Infact, he always plays the principal parts. They've retired here to Cardigan.' She went on, 'He's a light baritone. You've got to meet him, because you'll have someone to do duets with.'

So she snaffled him and we started doing duets together and all the old time... well, when I say 'old time' not that old, but Edwardian, you know standing by the piano where you'd have one foot on the stool. And all these lovely duets …

We performed all over. We were in great demand. We used to go round to a lot of the old people's clubs and homes and things like that, and anywhere that we were asked, really.

And so there were the three of us then. Eric would sing solos, and we'd do duets and then I'd sing a solo. If I've got someone with me, I can do the solo. And since then I've done shows on my own.

I have lived in various places. I emigrated to Canada as a young woman, but although I sang out there I didn't do what we're talking about now. I emigrated out there to my family that I had never met before, but they were all singers and singing in their church choir. They'd gone over to Canada so, when I went out, one of their big things was, 'It's Granddad's daughter who used to sing, it's his daughter and she sings too.'

But I didn't ever do any because I couldn't play the guitar then and I couldn't read music, but I'd always carry a tune. I came to Cardigan when I was twenty-nine. There was a big gap and I didn't actually sing. There isn't a family Welsh connection at all, unfortunately. But I've been here forty-five years.

When I first came to Cardigan, I was 29. The man who lived in this house, his wife had died and there were five children. The youngest was four and the oldest was sixteen, and I had two boys from a previous marriage. They came with me, so it was seven children to start off with. And then we had two girls, 'Hands and Feet' - one plays the piano and the other does feet - she's a chiropodist. That made a total of nine. Mr Painting, he was very musical. He played the fiddle and he had a nice light tenor voice.

My daughter Vicky was one of the first in the *B Natural* All-Women's Barber Shop Quartet and when she moved to London, of course, she had to drop out. Of all the children the music has sort of been concentrated into one. Mandy is the one who's really musical. The others all love music, but not exactly my sort of music.

I wouldn't say I don't like pop but I can't sing pop. They'd be more inclined to the sort of music that Mandy plays, than me.

I think music is so universal that whatever it is you do, you would be accepted.

I know when I've visited family abroad in Canada and South Africa, and New Zealand and Australia, I always take my guitar with me. I take my guitar up the flight path, and give it to a steward and say, 'Will you find a little corner for this with your coat?' and it always breaks the ice.

They say, 'Oh, what do you play? Oh!'

So, I've always taken my guitar with me and you always get invited out. It used to be a headache, because I couldn't tune it. If it had got out of tune, like if anybody had twiddled the knobs or anything, I'd have to get someone else to tune it up for me. And people couldn't believe that I could play, but I couldn't tune my own darn guitar!

In South Africa I was going down from the capital right down the coast, and it was a twenty-six hour train journey. You had to be on it overnight. And the train broke down about two or three hours before we were due to arrive in Durban .It was a really super train where you got your meals served and there was showers and, oh God, it was wonderful. We had to pull off into a siding to have this repair done. So we'd got a three-hour delay. And I was playing then for the people on the train.

If I give it serious thought, probably I may have liked to be famous. Everybody wants their moment of fame, don't they? But generally speaking …no, I don't… I've never given it any serious thought, anyhow.

Perhaps, if I had been young today, I'd have had a different attitude towards it. But you see, you don't really get a good living from singing, do you? Well, unless you are very good, and very lucky. Most people who sing tell you that it isn't their voice, it's been luck.

It's funny, when I go to Cardigan now I see so many people who know that I sing and they say, 'Are you still singing, Beryl?'

And I say, 'No, I'm not.'

And they say, 'Oh …'

And I say, 'Well, I'm not singing publicly, but I sing at home.'

If anybody asks me to sing, and Amanda is available, drop of a hat, we'll sing. It's like Mandy's being dragged along. She doesn't really like doing it, but if she wants me to do anything for her, she'll say, 'Come on Mum, we'll sing, shall we?' In other words, 'Let's get Mum in a good mood.'

SIWSANN GEORGE

SIWSANN GEORGE

Introduction

After travelling to the Rhondda to meet Siwsann, I felt that I had met a beautiful person. Some people have a natural beauty that shines out of them, even though they may be completely unaware of that beauty themselves. Siwsann contacted me by email and asked me if she could be included in my research because she wanted her contribution to song to be remembered alongside other Welsh women. Sadly, after a long struggle, Siwsann has now lost her fight against cancer. In dedication to her memory and in keeping my promise, her life is celebrated here.

I wasn't a natural to get up on stage although I always liked music. I remember the first album I had was *What Have They Done To The Rain?* which I still sing. It was about acid rain. I used to sing in the chapel, and the chapel would be full, absolutely bursting at the seams. I distinctly remember my brother and I doing an Eisteddfod together, singing together. Actually, we've never sung together since.

Lily Richards, my music teacher at school, who always behind me, she got HTV to choose me for a children's programme on the television, when I was in the 5th Form. I'd been on the television doing my first drama when I was eleven. They came round the classes in school and they picked people who were good at Welsh! Then they asked me back a couple of years later to do a drama, by Gwendolyn Parry, and it was the first programme in colour.

Then I eventually started winning the regional Eisteddfods. I've always had congenital heart disease, so I couldn't get to the ends of the sentences.

I started playing with a guitar and entering in the solo pop competition. I did actually get to the prelims of the Urdd. Then I went through a phase where I was sort of doing competitions. I think I wanted to prove to myself that I could win something. It was like I needed somebody to say, 'Yes, you have got a good voice, you have got abilities.' Because it's always the same ones who got the prizes and I wanted to show that I could do it as well.

The first time I went to college I started being really nervous going in for competitions. I'd had the second heart operation by then. I remember at one point I was in the toilets before going into a singing competition for the National Eisteddfod and I'd never been on stage there. This was for a folk solo and there are really strict, rigid rules. I've got some classic comments, 'You sung the wrong note in this bit...' But with folk music there's no right or wrong. By doing that, I did gain a bit of confidence. Folk singing is different, although I think it's still judged on whether you have a good classical voice, and not whether you have a good folk voice. I was in such a state in the toilet before going on to sing. I thought, 'This is ridiculous. I don't need this any more.' So I went to the Pan Celtic in Ireland, and I didn't get anywhere the first year, but then I won the second year. I went against fifteen other people from all the Celtic countries. I was nervous again, but I think it was the song that clinched it. I did a song about Aberfan, which I wrote. I translated it from the work of Sheila Douglas, from Scotland, and I think it just hit home. I also did one about the lighter side of mining, which I've recorded on my Traditional Songs of Wales CD. I won it that time and then there was two other times.

I just felt that I had recognition as a singer then, and I didn't bother doing any competitions after that. I didn't feel I needed to. I competed in *Song for Wales* doing the writing, the compositions and I've also judged twice; once in the BBC in Cardiff and once in Ireland. It's not a nice experience, judging, because it's just like I feel, 'Well, who am I to judge somebody anyway?'

Most of my life is framed around my different illnesses. They are like signposts. Where I'm going next? After my first heart operation, which was 1974, I had a year off and I worked in Cardiff, in a Welsh bookshop. That's how a lot of people know me, and I know lots of people because they used to come into the shop. It was the only Welsh bookshop and it also sold records. I worked there ten years altogether, right through my college days and everything. Then we started the band Mabsant from there. It was the '80s and folk was still very popular. I'd already started playing in the folk club in Cardiff. We concentrated on doing stuff from Glamorgan. We were doing songs which nobody else was doing, because it was needed to be done.

At that point St Fagans was set up as a government institution. You had to sign to say you wouldn't sing the material elsewhere because it would upset the distribution patterns for dialect studies. It was actually a museum, a real museum at the time. I'm not saying the people working there didn't want people to learn stuff, but certainly the government policy at that time, was that it was a 'Museum of Welsh folk life', not a living museum of Welsh folk life. And in fact, it was my idea .We did the first performance there. And then they had more and more people, and it just grew year after year. I am sure it would have been in the ethos somewhere, it wasn't just me thinking, but the thing is, it just happened. The time was right for it to happen. That was my ambition, to go and work in St Fagans, but I didn't have a high enough degree.

I studied Welsh and Classical Studies, but I had a lot of problems. My mother died when I was in second year in university, and I had migraines all through the exams, so I ended up with 'a pass'. I would have failed really, but it's just that with the work that I had done over the years, I managed to get through. One of my best friends was in prison for the language. I spent most of my second year protesting either in London or on CND things or Welsh Language Society things. I'm not saying now I was the best student either... And there's plenty of entertainment going on in Aberystwyth as well.

When I came back home from College, I couldn't find a job. I worked in Glamorgan archives for a bit, then I went round Cardiff looking to see if I could get a job as a bookseller. But the thing is, you can't get weekends off and we were getting asked to go to folk festivals. I was thinking of going nursing, and I thought, 'That's not going to work either, if I want to carry on singing.' So then I went to college for music and drama, for a year, doing the Diploma in Drama.

I worked for Cardiff Broadcasting for a year. I used to do a folk programme called *Taplas*, which is now the magazine. I let them have the name for the magazine because they axed the programme. The people in London said that there wasn't enough money being made on the records, because it was a community radio station and not playing a lot of pop. It's found its balance now, but they sort of went right the other way. They got rid of anybody who was doing anything community and so most of them got jobs at the Beeb. I thought I wanted to carry on performing. I was doing a weekly magazine programme, called *Ffair Caerdydd*. I used have a different society on every week.

After that I did a teaching diploma for a year. I went teaching for a year but then I thought, 'If I don't get this job, I'm going on the road.' I did the probationary year and another year in Maesteg. And then I went on the road with *Mabsant*. Stewart, who I was then living with, moved down here and we went travelling together and singing. We used to go for £25 per night down to the southeast and to people like *Folk on Tap* in the Portsmouth area. They used to arrange that you'd play one club every night in an area. You can't do that anymore, because they tend to say that you can't play within a 50 mile radius, but in those days people just had their own club in their own area. If people wanted to see you more than once, they'd travel to the next one. We'd cover a whole area, and we'd stay with one person, one of the organisers. Eventually, we'd feel like they were like second homes in a way. Very kind people put us up, sometimes for a couple of weeks.

I've always been very aware that I haven't got the figure and the looks to be a pop star. I think that I can get away with being a folk singer with my looks, but I can't get away with being a pop star. When you see these pop star programmes, I feel really sad for the young people that are wanting to take part. It's such a lot of pressure to do that and all the image conscious thing. You actually do what you can do, you know. You don't realize at the time. I've got quite small hands, not very small but I've got quite small hands. I've never been able to bar very well on the guitar. So I used a capo. You adapt all the time to what you can do. It depends what you can do.

A woman can decide that she's not going to have children, but it doesn't always work out. So you've got to stop and accommodate children into your life as well. And then put it on hold, and your career on hold. The illness has stopped me, rather than the having a family. Although I had to do things in a different way, like I wouldn't have been able to travel so much...

The tumour has gone down to half size of what it was. But my stomach's been playing up as well, so I don't know. It's nothing like it was. I can't have any more surgery now. If I can do things, then I do them. People just fill in the gaps don't they? It's part of the fun really.

It means a lot to me being Welsh because that's where I'm born, but it can be double-sided. I do find it frustrating sometimes because there's a lot of things that need progression in Wales. We're a bit behind the times on some aspects.

I think song has kept me alive. It's been a kind of survival thing because...well it keeps you going doesn't it? It gives me motivation to carry on really. I'm lucky that I've got it. It's not something that was forced on me as a child. 'You have to join the local choir, children's choir...' Well, in fact, it was the other way round. I don't think my parents encouraged us to do that much, because they didn't think it was a proper job... wasn't a proper thing to do, you know.

ACKNOWLEDGEMENTS

There are so many people to thank for making my vision *Heaven Scent* a reality.

The *biggest thanks* go to all the women who have kindly given of their time and their life histories. I might never have found *the songstress* without all the people who responded to my adverts and flyers, so thank you to all of them.

Thankyou to Roy Sear and to Mick Themes, for offering long lists of contacts and to Women in Tune, who placed an internet notice. In addition, thank you to my friend Jeff Rees, who gave me my first list of contacts and offered encouragement when all this was just a seed. He also proofed for me at the end, coming full circle.

Thankyou to *The Arts Council of Wales* for believing in my work and awarding me with a small grant. This gave my confidence a great boost and enabled me to dedicate my time to carrying out the research.

Thanks to all the people who helped with the transcriptions, in particular Delyth Byrne and Christine Foley.

Thankyou to Moira Andrew; *The Travelling Poet*. Moira has been an inspiration to me since we first worked together some years ago and has influenced the way I have structured my own creative life. I thank her for being a light when I was in a dark place and for helping with edits; for teaching me how to make transcripts look bookish!

Thankyou to St.Fagan's Museum Archive Department and to Bridgend Library.

Thankyou to the Williams family and in particular, Maria Jane.

Sometimes people meet and are a constant source of mutual support . Luckily for me, I met such a person: Mr. Jeff Beer seventeen years ago, I put an advert in a music shop window in Bridgend saying, *'Experienced singer looking for working band.'* Jeff rang and I auditioned for *Clouds over Egypt*. Needless to say, I got the job and we've been soul mates ever since. Thanks for all your support, Jeff.

Thankyou Lillian Connor, my Guardian Angel.

SPECIAL MENTIONS

There are three women to whom I would like to a give special mention.
These are excerpts from their websites.

The first is Moira Andrew as mentioned in the acknowledgements

When I moved to Bristol, I became head of a primary school. One day two of my Year 5 girls challenged me to produce a poem for their classroom wall - and that's how I started writing for children. I remarried and moved to Wales, left full-time teaching and started a new career as a freelance writer. I'm lucky to be able to combine my teaching experience and an interest in artwork with my love of writing. My first book for Belair is called 'Language in Colour'. It was published in 1989 and is still going strong. I have six more Belair/Folens books in publication. I'm a 'jobbing writer', accepting all kinds of writing opportunities, but my heart really lies in poetry aimed at an adult audience.

The second is Linda Simmonds from the band Allan Yn Y Fan.
Linda plays Bodrhan on the *Heaven Scent* single.

Linda was responsible for the organisation and promotion for Islwyn Folk Club and festivals. She is a Director of Pontardawe festival having volunteered as a back stage manager for many years. Linda plays keyboards, guitar, mandolin and bodrhan. She has\ left behind the glamour of newspaper journalism for a senior press officer role with the Welsh Assembly.

The third is Sian James who played harp on Irish Lilt, the second track on the *Heaven Scent* single.

Music has always been an inextricable part of my life. I was surrounded by music from a very early age and was put on the stage by my mother at the age of three to compete in our local Eisteddfodau. I began learning the piano at the age of six, the violin at eight and the harp at eleven. At fourteen, I began my concert career singing traditional songs as part of a harp trio, along with solo performances to my own harp accompaniment. Soon I began composing songs and creating my own arrangements of traditional songs, and discovered that improvising and creating at the piano and harp brought me enormous enjoyment. Following these formative years my professional life has been divided between an acting career and music.

CHERYL BEER MERCHANDISE

BIBLIOGRAPHY

TALES FROM TWO VALLEYS
Community poetry book exploring local folk history
Excellence Award from Wales Youth Agency

CELTIC HEROINES
Community poetry book celebrating
Welsh Celtic women and Goddesses
Nominated for Excellence Award

THE AMAZING ADVENTURES OF SUPERBOO
Children and adults alike will love this story book

DISCOGRAPHY

UP CLOSE & PERSONAL *Cassette EP*

JUST ANOTHER JUDAS *CD Album*
Folking.com Album of the Month

BEAUTIFUL BEARDED LADY *Compilation Album*

LITTLE FISH : BARE BONE SONGS
HMV Choice Album of the Month

SONGWRITER'S GUIDE TO INDIA
Fundraising Album for the children of Sri Sai Community School

WOMEN4ZIMBABWE
Fundraising Album for The Zimbabwe Academy of Music for Women

HEAVEN SCENT :
THE HISTORY OF THE WELSH SONGSTRESS
Fundraising Single for Breast Cancer Research, Velindre Hospital, Cardiff

www.cherylbeer.com

SOUNDBITES CD

Welcome to your complimentary gift, a soundbite CD which enables you to listen to the spoken word and singing voices of *The Welsh Songstress*.

Where *live* recordings are included, these were taken at the time of interview. Other pre-recorded songs are taken from the discs and cassettes recorded by the women. If you would like further information about the work of any of the welsh songstresses, please email via www.cherylbeer.com

RUNNING ORDER

Heather Jones singing a track from her new album *Hwyrnos*
Kath Allsop singing *True Friends* from her album *Love an' all that*
Marjorie Jones singing with The Heath Town's Women's Guild from their CD *Salute to Her Majesty*
Gerri Smith singing *Every Time We Say Goodbye*
Kate Strudwick playing with her band *Allan Yn Y Fan*
Lynne Gent singing *Save the Child* from a fundraising cassette
Ruth Exell Stevenson speaking.
Jen Wilson performing a track from her album
Twelve Poems: A Jazz Suite by Jen Wilson
Anita Whitehouse singing a track from *Still Singing at Seventy*
Frankie Armstrong singing from her album *Lovely on the water*
Helen Davies singing live *Sparkle like Diamonds*
Buddug Lloyd Roberts singing on her cassette *Helo Blant*
Valerie Manning Singers performing *Any Dream Will Do*
Heather Jones singing *Coed y wein calon* funded by **Teleri Gray**
Pat Smith & Mick Themes singing live
Hawys Glyn James singing & playing live
Siwsann George singing from her CD *Trevithick's Train*
Beryl Painting with Amanda Painting singing & playing live

 Cheryl Beer performing *Heaven Scent*.
A fundraising single for breast cancer research
at Velindre Hospital, Cardiff.
Available from www.cherylbeer.com

NB. Cd was mastered before Beattie Pugh was interviewed